TMH Professional: Cracking the IT Interview Series

Cracking IT Campus Interviews

Other Titles in this Series

- **Cracking System Software Interview**
  SG Ganesh and Sandya Mannarswamy

- **Cracking the C, C++ and JAVA Interview, 2e**
  SG Ganesh and Subhash KU

- **Cracking the QTP Interview**
  Siva Koti Reddy K

- **Cracking the IT Interview, 2e**
  Balasubramaniam et al.

TMH Professional: Cracking the IT Interview Series

Cracking IT Campus Interviews

Deepa Jain

IBM Software

Tata McGraw Hill Education Private Limited

NEW DELHI

McGraw-Hill Offices

New Delhi New York St Louis San Francisco Auckland Bogotá Caracas Kuala Lumpur Lisbon London Madrid Mexico City Milan Montreal San Juan Santiago Singapore Sydney Tokyo Toronto

Tata McGraw-Hill

Published by Tata McGraw Hill Education Private Limited,
7 West Patel Nagar, New Delhi 110 008

ISBN (13): 978-1-25-906387-9
ISBN (10): 1-25-906387-9

Vice President and Managing Director—Asia-Pacific Region: *Ajay Shukla*
Publishing Manager—Professional: *Praveen Tiwari*
Editorial Researcher—Science, Technology and Computing: *Sushil Gupta*
Sr. Copy Editor: *Neha Sharma*
Manager—Production: *Sohan Gaur*
Asst. General Manager—Sales and Business Development—Professional: *S Girish*
Deputy Marketing Manager—Science, Technology and Computing: *Rekha Dhynai*
General Manager—Production: *Rajender P Ghansela*
Manager—Production: *Reji Kumar*

Typeset at Text-o-Graphics, B-1/56 Arawali Apartment, Sector 34, Noida 201 301 and printed at Rajkamal Electric Press, Plot No. 2, Phase IV, HSIIDC, Kundli, Sonepat, Haryana - 131028

Cover Printer: Rajkamal Electric Press

Cover Designer: Mukul Khattar

RCCLCRXHRBBLY

The McGraw·Hill Companies

To

My Family

Preface

Hello Readers, I am happy that you are looking at this book and hopefully reading through. Let me tell how and why this book was born.

Why I Wrote This Stuff

This book is based on my first-hand interview experiences as a student a few years back and as a campus interviewer now. As an interviewer, I used to jot down my experiences with the students soon after every event was over, trying to recollect what the interviewees had said, what I had felt and what my colleagues thought about them. It was initially intended for improving my own skills as an interviewer. After some time, it occurred to me that I had collected a few interesting interview stories that could benefit the other interviewees as well. So, I decided to pen down those stories in the form of a book, and this is how this book was ideated.

For Whom the Book is

One of the important parameters we consider before applying for admission into any engineering college is its placement record. This book is a placement guide meant mainly for engineering students.

This book is basically meant for those students who start worrying about the placements even before completing 1st year of engineering, who get nervous at the thought of interviews, and who spend a lot of money on coaching institutes claiming to offer magic formulae for succeeding in interviews. And as we all know, this group forms the vast majority of engineering students.

This book brings to you real interview transcripts.

Takeaways From The Book

You can learn how an answer begets a question, how an interviewer can see through fake answers, what all tricks are applied by the interviewer to get an insight into the student's capabilities.

The sixth sense is the strongest sense one has. You are in a best position to understand a situation by being witness to it in person rather than hearing a third party account. That is why we bring to you the real interviews. You can swim through them to gauge the depths, currents and undercurrents on the antennae of sixth sense. A last/fourth scene is still provided at the end of each interview to hear the interviewer's perception about the just completed interview.

This book will help you take a chill pill by familiarizing you with the real event, like a mock drill and help you better prepare for the actual ordeal—well it won't remain an ordeal anymore.

How To Enjoy This Book

Role play is the best way to enjoy the experiences shared in the book. One of you can assume the role of an interviewer ready to grill the interviewee who can be a friend and avenge him on a past practical joke.

Thanks

Thanks to TMH for accepting me as the first time author, making me feel special from the first day we met each other and guiding me throughout.

Thanks to IBM for providing me with an opportunity to interview students.

Deepa Jain

Contents

1

Electrical's Sarin Appears for Neura Tech

SCENE 1

A hushed discussion is going on among a group of anxious-looking students and the most anxious looking lad is at the center of this discussion. An enthusiastic volunteer comes over and addresses this lad, "Oye chill yaar, by Lady Luck, the only girl in the Neura Tech team is going to be your interviewer! Just wear that cute smile of yours throughout and you would be through for sure." The group breaks into an instant celebration.

SCENE 2

The interviewee is knocking at the door of Room No. IV …

Interviewee (*smiling*): May I come in, M'am?

Interviewer (*smiling*): Yes, please come in Sarin. Have a seat please!

Sarin (*still smiling nervously*): Thanks M'am.

Interviewer (*encouraging*): How are you doing Sarin? I hope you got a chance to finish your lunch.

Sarin (*enthusiastic*): Yes M'am, I did. Thanks!

Interviewer: How did the test and the GD go for you?

Sarin (*happily*): M'am, the test was easy as I had practiced a lot. The GD went fine, it was on euthanasia, as you know a very hot topic right now, so the group got a bit aggressive.

(Interviewer to herself: I asked specifically about his performance and he is talking about the group! Trying to be smart, ah! Anyways he is the top scorer in the written test, so I hope to see some spark in him.)

Interviewer (*apparently agreeing*): Yes, you are right, Sarin. Tell me something about Sarin!

Sarin (*confused*): M'am, to tell you something about Sa ... oh yes, yes M'am, my name is Sarin. I am a final-year electrical engineering student at the Copernicus Institute of Technology. My percentage till sixth semester is 77. I completed my class XII from Allahabad and scored 94 percent in the CBSE exams. I have a younger brother, who is studying to be a CA. My father is in defense and I have lived at many places in India. My hobbies are photography and playing cricket.

(Interviewer, smiling inwardly: Boy, you have learnt your introduction by heart and yet you got as confused as a cow on astroturf when I changed a simple word in the question! And you didn't speak a word about engineering! But your CV has a project description where you have helped in the electrification of rural areas, which looks very interesting indeed.)

Interviewer (*prodding further*): What are your favorite subjects?

Sarin (*confidently*): Power Systems, Transmission, and Electrical Machines.

Interviewer (*curious*): All right. I can see that you have done an interesting project where you have saved the cost for rural electrification by 50 percent. Tell me more about this project.

Sarin (*excited*): M'am, right now the cost of electrification is very high and because of that many of our villages are still in dark. We have used earth as the return wire and saved the cost of the return conductor. In this way all village folk would be able to afford the cost of electricity and it would even help agriculture.

Interviewer: Please continue with your description of the cost reduction.

Sarin (*smiling again*): OK, M'am. As we have used earth as the return wire, so there is no need for another return wire. This will reduce cost. When the cost of installation will go down, more rural areas would be electrified sooner. In this manner ... hmm ... that is the description of our project. We have done it as a group of ... umm ... five students from our class.

Interviewer (*still confused*): Sarin, I have already read in your CV what you just said. I did not understand how you have made earth as the return. I have basically two questions still on my mind: first, how did you reduce earth's resistance so that your losses still remained negligible and it could serve as an effective conductor; second, if that happens, wouldn't anyone walking on ground get electrocuted? And what will happen when a farmer is irrigating his land. Can you please explain me these two things?

Sarin (*half-heartedly*): No M'am, no. That is not what we have done. We cannot do that. Actually if you see it in more detail, then in city areas there is a three-phase power supply. Many industries need a three-phase supply. But in rural areas, we can do with a single-phase power supply. So we have recommended for a single-phase power supply for the rural areas that are yet to be electrified.

Interviewer (*disagreeing*): But how does this explanation fit into your project description?

Sarin (*upset*): M'am, for three-phase supply, you need three conductors. For a single-phase supply, you will need just one live conductor. So that will save the cost of wire.

Interviewer (*completely disillusioned*): Fine, I understand that now. But it makes me wonder what you have really done as a part of your project implementation in that case. And I request you to talk to me like an electrical engineer as by education, I am one myself.

Sarin (*crestfallen*): I thought you were from IT background and I was wondering how you were asking those questions. To be honest M'am, it is just the start of the eighth semester and we have not yet finalized our final-year project. This cost-saving analysis, we had done as part of our sixth-semester project.

(Interviewer, obviously very angry: I could have rejected you right away, but for your confession and good percentage and communication, I am giving you another chance.)

Interviewer (*changing topic*): All right then Sarin, let's talk about your favorite subject, Electrical Machines. Explain to me the principle and working of a generator.

Sarin (*calm*): M'am, a generator converts mechanical energy into electrical energy. It works on Faraday's principle of electromagnetic induction. If a conductor is moved across a magnetic field, current is induced in it. Now about the working of the generator, it consists of a rotor and a stator. The rotor is connected to a source of power like a steam turbine. The stator is connected to the load generally.

Interviewer: It would be good if you could draw the block diagram on this paper.

Sarin: Sure, M'am.

(Sarin draws the diagram and explains further)

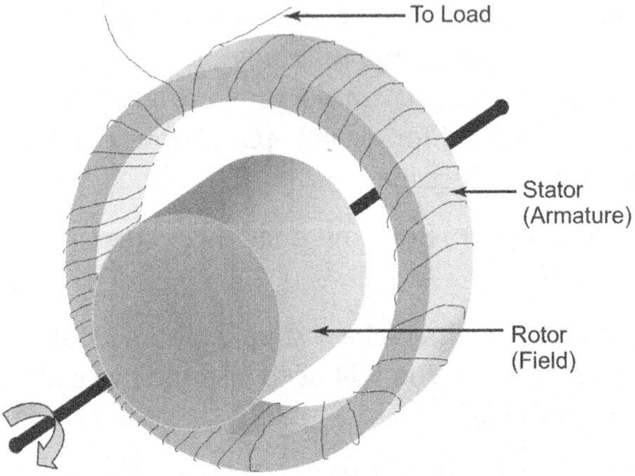

In this diagram, the armature or the winding is the stator and the magnetic field is the rotor. Generally a smaller set of winding is used to produce the field. To make it simple, we can assume that it is a permanent magnet. As you can see, the armature is connected to a load. This particular arrangement of rotor and stator makes the magnetic flux cut across the whole of the armature and produce more current.

Interviewer: Sarin, what type of generator is this?

Sarin: Umm … type as in?

Interviewer: AC, DC, phase …

Sarin: Yes, it is … it is DC single phase, sorry M'am, it is single-phase AC generator.

Interviewer: Are you sure about that?

Sarin (*confidently*): Yes, you have to split the armature lead by a split ring to produce DC. The direction of field and current will change after half rotation, so you need to connect to the other end of the armature to keep the direction of the current same.

Interviewer (*smiling*): I like that confidence. Any other difference in the design of a DC generator?

Sarin (*unsure*): Hmm … the armature is the rotor and the field becomes the stator.

Interviewer: I remember you saying a conductor should be moved across a field for induction, so why don't you make the stator as a solid iron core? Also, windings do get burnt routinely.

Sarin (*still unsure*): It must be because of the eddy currents … a … that we use thin wire.

Interviewer (*grinning*): Hmm … suppose the generator is on, casing is all open and you accidently touch the winding. What will happen?

Sarin (*shifting in the chair and gulping*): No, not sure M'am!

Interviewer (*smiling*): You must be thinking, "What type of an interview is this? I came all prepared for an IT interview and this person is not asking me anything on that." Am I right?

Sarin (*grinning*): No M'am, not like that.

Interviewer: Good then! Photography being your hobby, what type of pictures do you click?

Sarin (*smiling*): Nature photography mostly. I like to capture flying birds from a close distance, flowering buds too. And of course I take my girlfriend's pics.

Interviewer (*objectively*): Do you play around with the flash?

Sarin (*excited*): Absolutely! And I have to turn it off most of the times to click birds.

Interviewer: Do you know what the single most important component of a camera flash circuit is?

Sarin (*baffled*): Hmm … it must be the … umm … flash light itself! Is that correct, M'am?

Interviewer (*smiling*): I would call the transformer as more important.

Sarin (*curious*): Why M'am?

Interviewer (*smiling*): Find out for yourself when you go back!

(Interviewer, sadly : His apparent interests are electrical machines and photography and still he does not even know that transformer is used to step up a few volts of the battery to over a kilovolt to produce the flash discharge! At the same time, he explained a generator's theory! Let me ask him more questions before I can decide anything.)

Interviewer: What do you know about C language?

Sarin: I have used like loops, pointers, …umm… arrays, structures…

Interviewer: What is recursion?

Sarin: Recursion is like calling self. For example, I write a function CheckPrime which takes a number as an argument. Inside this function, I make a call to the same function with a different argument, and then that becomes a recursive call. I will write it down.

```
public void CheckPrime(int num)
{
int n = num;
int val;
/*some lines of code*/
val = CheckPrime (n - 1);
/*more code*/
return 1;
}
```

Interviewer: Can you please explain the first line of the code that you have written?

Sarin: Yes M'am, this is the CheckPrime function definition. The keyword public means it is accessible from outside. Void means it does not return any value. Sorry M'am, it should be int and not void as it returns an integer value.

public ~~void~~ int CheckPrime(int num)

Interviewer: I think public is defined in C++ and it works in your programs as most of the compilers used are the C++ compilers. I make a small change to your program as this. What will happen? Which type of error will it throw?

~~val = CheckPrime (n - 1);~~

val = CheckPrime (n);

Sarin (*confused*): Hmm … It shouldn't give any error …

Interviewer: Are you sure about that?

Sarin: Let me check again … I don't think there is any syntax error. Oh yes, it will result in an infinite loop!

Interviewer: Apart from this change that I made, do you see any other way to make this program run forever?

Sarin (*anticipating*): Maybe…

(He analyzes the code twice)

Sarin (*smiling*): Yes M'am, if you delete this part of the code, it will run forever.

/**/

public ~~void~~ int CheckPrime(int num)

{

int n = num;

int val;

~~/*some lines of code*/~~

val = CheckPrime(n - 1);

/*more code*/

}

/**/

Interviewer: Do you know how recursion works?

Sarin: I did not get that.

Interviewer: Have you heard about stacks?

Sarin: Yes, it is Last In First Out.

Interviewer: Does recursion implementation need a stack usage?

Sarin: Yes, it does. It stores the latest argument on stack top and makes a function call again. Actually M'am, in that scenario the above program will run till it runs out of stack memory.

Interviewer (*smiling*): Yes, that is what I was looking for. Please write a bubble sort code for sorting the following.

5, 2, 9, 4, 8, 6, 3, 1, 7, 0

Sarin: M'am, these numbers are in array or list format?

Interviewer: Whatever you are comfortable with. You can assume in array format.

(Interviewer to herself: He seems to know at least a little bit of C which is good. He has dropped some of the arrogance also. But let me check his general awareness a little more as I still cannot whole-heartedly decide to select him.)

(Sarin writes the program in the meanwhile)

```
/***********************************************************/

#include <stdio.h>

void main()
{
    int arr[] = {5, 2, 9, 4, 8, 6, 3, 1, 7, 0};
    int  initial, i, j;

    for (i = 0; i < 9; i++)
    {
        for (j=0;j < (9-i);j++)
        {
            if (arr[j] > arr[j+1])
            {
                initial = arr[j];
                arr[j] = arr[j+1];
                arr[j+1] = initial;
            }
        }  }
    printf("\n Sorted Array is : \n ");
```

```
    for (i = 0; i < 10; i++)
    printf("%d", arr[i]);
}
/*************************************************************/
```

Interviewer: Sarin, please explain me the code line by line.

Sarin: M'am, the first line is to include the printf and scanf functions code from the standard input and output header file. The next line is a call to the main function. Every program needs to include one call to this function. Next is defined an array variable "arr" of integer type.

Sorting the array by the bubble sort algorithm requires two loops. First is the outer loop, which has a nested second loop. The sorting proceeds like this:

1. The first pass compares all the elements of the array, here it does nine comparisons like this:
   - 1.1 Take the first element of the array and compare it with the next element. Swap if required to bring the greater number to right side in the array.
   - 1.2 Take the second element of the array and compare it with the next element. Swap if required to bring the greater number to right side in the array.

Array To Be Sorted

5	2	9	4	8	6	3	1	7	0
1st Value	2nd Value	3rd Value	4th Value	5th Value	6th Value	7th Value	8th Value	9th Value	10th Value

First Pass, First Comparison

< ? >

5	2	9	4	8	6	3	1	7	0
1st Value	2nd Value	3rd Value	4th Value	5th Value	6th Value	7th Value	8th Value	9th Value	10th Value

First Pass, First Swap

2	5	9	4	8	6	3	1	7	0
1st Value	2nd Value	3rd Value	4th Value	5th Value	6th Value	7th Value	8th Value	9th Value	10th Value

   - 1.3 Repeat this process till the last second element of the array, in this example, till the ninth element.
   - 1.4 This completes the first pass and we have the largest number at the rightmost position in the array.

End of First Pass, Largest Value Bubbled to Top

2	5	4	8	6	3	1	7	0	9
1st Value	2nd Value	3rd Value	4th Value	5th Value	6th Value	7th Value	8th Value	9th Value	10th Value

2. The second pass compares (n – 1) left elements of the array, here it compares eight times like the first-pass comparison.

End of Second Pass, Second Largest Value Bubbled to Top

2	4	5	6	3	1	7	0	8	9
1st Value	2nd Value	3rd Value	4th Value	5th Value	6th Value	7th Value	8th Value	9th Value	10th Value

3. n – 1 passes are completed in this manner to completely sort the array.

Interviewer: That was absolutely correct. Do you know the complexity of this algorithm?

Sarin: It is … hmm … it's n^2.

Interviewer (*smiling*): Can you please explain to me how that value of n^2 is determined?

Sarin: Sure, M'am. I will first write it down and then explain.

Total number of comparisons done:

$(n - 1) + (n - 2) + (n - 3) + \cdots + (n - (n - 1)) = n(n - 1)/2$

Total number of swaps done in worst-case scenario:

$(n - 1) + (n - 2) + (n - 3) + \cdots + (n - (n - 1)) = n(n - 1)/2$

Total number of operations:

$[n(n - 1)/2] + [n(n - 1)/2] = n^2 - n$

Complexity (when n > 10) ≈ n^2

Sarin: So as you can see, sorting basically involves comparison and swap operations. There are approximately n^2 operations involved.

Interviewer (*impressed*): Wow! You have been the first person in this campus season who could justify this complexity so clearly. Are you genuinely interested in computers?

(Interviewer to herself: Boy, you really did not mention anything about your interests in computers till I asked you. Imagine if I had rejected you for your not so flattering electrical knowledge!)

Sarin: Yes M'am, I feel quite comfortable with programming logic. I have also taught the basics of C to my friends and juniors.

Interviewer (*delighted*): That's very good to know! Do you have a PC or a laptop?

Sarin: I have a PC.

Interviewer: On what operating systems do you work? Windows or Linux?

Sarin: It is Windows XP.

Interviewer: OK. Is it a multitasking multiuser system?

Sarin: Hmm ... it is multitasking for sure. Multiuser ... We can create multiple user profiles but not sure if all of them can be logged into the machine at one time. I don't think it is a multiuser system in the real sense!

Interviewer: I want media player on my system to be automatically started at 5 every evening. Can you please help me?

Sarin: Well, I can write a batch file and check time in that and put a command to run media player exe at 5 PM. Then this file needs to be put in the startup programs. That's it!

Interviewer (*smiling*): Is there a simpler way to do it?

Sarin (*confused*): Not sure, M'am...

Interviewer: Have you seen the Windows scheduler? You can schedule programs there.

Sarin: I was not aware of that, M'am.

Interviewer: No issues. Tell me something interesting that you have learnt about computers.

Sarin (*grinning*): There are two things that I have learnt and felt very happy. I used to see the system date getting automatically updated every time I started my system and used to wonder how that happened. Then in one of our subjects, Microprocessors, I learnt about the quartz crystal system clock. But then, storing that generated value in memory needs power. Then we searched online and found out that a lithium ion battery is used to power the basic system setup when the mains power is off.

The second thing was working with the LAN setup group for our first-year hostel. I was the only non-IT guy in that group and learnt how it is practically set up, all about switches, router configuration, and passwords, etc. It was an even more enriching experience.

Interviewer (*smiling*): All right Sarin, I see you have worked even outside your engineering discipline and that's very good! I have no more questions for you. Do you have any questions?

Sarin: Yes M'am, I would want to know about the joining location, if selected.

Interviewer: You would get the option to specify your location preference in the form that the selected candidates will be asked to fill in.

Sarin: Thanks, M'am.

Interviewer: Thanks for your time, Sarin. Have a good day!

SCENE 3

The interviewer marks a Tech Select against Sarin's name in the list. She puts an asterisk over attitude and recommends an attitude-based HR evaluation. She grades his discipline knowledge as Average and adds a comment that it is very theoretical in nature. Computer basics and programming skills is graded Good with a comment, "Good programming aptitude." He gets a Very Good grade in communication with a remark, "Articulates well and quite fluent in English."

SCENE 4

A colleague congratulates the interviewer for her first selection of the day and prods her to share Sarin's exceptional qualities.

The interviewer almost blurts out, "He was plain lucky, very lucky!" You know he has such a pathetic knowledge of his subject though he is among the toppers. He has a good memory that really helps him in cramming for his papers. And to crown it all, he thinks we are dumb. And he has been selected by me; he was lucky that I could digest all this insult and not order him out immediately.

Then I discovered that he is good at computers. He fared quite well if you look at just the computer-based questions. That seems to be his real interest, but like all lost souls he has never done any true SWOT analysis.

His real strength and interest lies in computers and programming logic but he is blissfully unaware of the fact or at least I thought so as he did not care to mention any word on it till I asked him.

Has mentioned photography as his interest in his CV but does not even understand the electrical components of a camera. On that I really gave him the benefit of doubt. I thought he might not be interested in electrical and for that reason cannot see his surroundings in that light. It's possible that he had to opt for a better college than a course of interest. Not that I took a confirmation on that, but just had let the doubt live and benefit him.

Another reason for his selection was his communication skill. It's a rare privilege to get such a fluent speaker and good articulator at fresher level.

To cut the long story short, he is a very good communicator and programmer and is genuinely interested in computers. What more could I ask for!

2

Computers' Ravi and FuzzySoft

SCENE 1

In the computer center lobby, among a herd of nervous wrecks waiting for their turns is a very simple looking guy sitting calm and composed. As the interviewer walks across the lobby, this serene face does not escape his notice and he immediately concludes that this boy cannot be appearing for today's event. Wondering who he might be, he enters the room allotted to him and gets busy with three interviews for the next 40 minutes. Then he looks at the last profile in his list and calls for Ravi. He is too tired and bored by now to go through Ravi's CV lying at his table. The only thought playing upon his mind is to wrap up for the day within the next 10 minutes and to go shopping for the famous soft toys he has promised his daughter as a penance for not spending another Sunday with her.

SCENE 2

A soft voice greets the interviewer; he returns the greeting and asks the owner of the voice to sit down.

Interviewer (*uninterested*): You are Ravi, right? Tell me about yourself.

(*As the interviewer looks up from his cell phone at the person sitting across the table, he is stunned to find the same serene face he had seen in the lobby and starts browsing through the CV as Ravi starts speaking.*)

Ravi (*warmly and naturally*): Sir, I am Ravi Sunder, a fourth-year Computer Science student at the Copernicus Institute of Technology. I have a good understanding of my subjects and my strength lies in my programming skills. I have won seven programming contests during the last three years. Apart from computers, I have a keen interest in music and literature. Occasionally, I write short stories and poems. I enjoy long walks with friends. I completed my schooling from Swadesh Gram, Ma …

(*Interviewer notices that though Ravi has spoken about his strengths and accomplishments which are definitely extraordinary by a student's standards, yet there has been no air of arrogance or flaunt in his tone.*)

Interviewer (*impulsively*): Swadesh Gram is a beautiful but remotely located town! How do you speak such refined English?

Ravi (*grimly*): Sir, I owe my education to my father who used to get the best books home for me. He also introduced me to BBC News when I was in third standard. My father, those books and the BBC News have been my English teachers.

Interviewer (*delighted*): Ravi, can you please also share the secret of the extremely good marks that you have always managed to score!

Ravi (*smiling*): Sir, the secret is group study. We are a group of eight friends who collectively study and teach each other all the six subjects every semester. We always find it easiest to understand and remember concepts through explaining them to others, rather than learning by self.

Interviewer (*smiling*): That's absolutely wonderful! We would love to recruit all eight of you! Are others appearing for this event?

Ravi (*smiling*): Thanks for your generous offer, Sir. I am sorry to say that they have already been selected by the earlier companies.

Interviewer: Didn't you appear for them?

Ravi: No Sir, I was waiting for the FuzzySoft event as my work area aligns with the work being done by your company.

Interviewer (*skeptical*): Are you planning for an MS?

Ravi (*honest*): Yes Sir, I am. But I am not in a position to pursue further studies right now. I will have to work for three to four years to be able to afford my tuition fees.

(*The interviewer is highly touched by this young man's words. He decides to select Ravi and even makes a mental note to push for his inclusion in his very own team.*

Yet sad as he has become, he decides to bring about a change in the mood of the interview.)

Interviewer (*lively*): Ravi, may I get the pleasure of hearing you play the mouth organ?

Ravi (*happily*): Sure Sir, I will fetch my harmonica from the hostel as soon as this interview gets over.

Interviewer (*smiling*): That would not be required. Can you please pretend play right now?

Ravi (*smiling*): All right Sir, I will try. I will play "Happy B'Day." Would that be fine?

Interviewer: Yes, perfect!

(*Ravi gets out from his seat, brings his hands close to his mouth, pretends to hold a harmonica and starts imitating the melodious beats through his vocal chords. As his performance gets over, the interviewer claps with joy.*)

Interviewer (*enthralled*): Superb! Wonderful! Surreal!

Ravi (*happily*): Thank you, Sir!

(*The interviewer offers Ravi some water and he accepts gladly. There is a pause for a couple of minutes during which the interviewer wishes Ravi great luck and appreciates his talent further.*)

Interviewer: Congratulations, Ravi! I am pleased to inform that you have cleared the HR round. Are you ready for a technical round now?

Ravi (*gladly*): Thank you, Sir! Yes, I am all set for the technical round.

Interviewer: Tell me about the latest programming contest you won.

Ravi: The latest contest was more like a rapid-fire round where the seven finalists were given a problem and they had to give a solution in the least possible time. There were six such questions given, each at an interval of 5 minutes. The time taken by each to submit a solution was noted down and added up. The candidate with the least time and maximum correct solutions was to win.

The very first problem given was about writing an infinite program without using any loop in the shortest time. I could finish it in 25 seconds by recursively calling main. The recursive call of main function was appreciated by the judges also as no one else had used the same logic.

```
/*****************************************************/
main()
{
main();
}
/*****************************************************/
```

Interviewer: Shall I share a secret with you Ravi?

Ravi: Yes Sir, please do.

Interviewer: You have been the first student I met who has written a working program with a call to the main function. Please continue.

Ravi: Sir, The next problem was about displaying the first n numbers of the Fibonacci series. I found this straightforward and could immediately think of the x = x + y and y = x + y iterations logic to generate the series. On this I had to do a couple of trial runs to set the count of numbers to be displayed. I could complete this in almost 3 minutes.

```
/*****************************************************/
#include <stdio.h>
/*Display a series of n Fibonacci numbers */
void main()
{
    float x = 0, y = 1, count, i;

    printf("\n Enter count \n");
    scanf("%f", &count);
/*****************************************************/
    printf("\n Fibonacci Series for %.0f numbers is : \n 0 %.0f ", count, y);
    for (i=1;(i < (count -1));i+=2)
    {
        x = x + y;
        y = x + y;
        printf("%.0f", x);
        if ((i+1) < (count-1)) printf("%.0f", y);
```

```
    }
}
/*************************************************/
```

Interviewer: What made you choose the float data type over the integer data type?

Ravi: Sir, the upper limit for integers is 2 to the power of 16 minus 1. That would have limited the maximum count for the series. My decision to choose the float data type and then to use a %.0f format modifier to suppress the decimal part was the best part about my program. In this round, few others could complete their programs in less than 2 minutes but they faced many run-time limitations.

Next we were asked to write a program to find the smallest prime number greater than a given number, which is best optimized for performance.

It took me long to write this program and I somehow managed to complete it in 5 minutes. But surprisingly it turned out to be the best-optimized program. I will write it down and highlight the main performance points.

```
/*************************************************/
#include <stdio.h>

/*Smallest Prime Number greater than a given number optimized for
performance*/

int IsPrime(long unsigned number)
{
    long unsigned num = number, i = 0, z = 0;

    if (! int(num % 2))
        return 0;
    if (! int(num % 3))
        return 0;
    if (! int(num % 5))
```

```
            return 0;
        for (i = 5; i < num/2 ; )
        {
            //printf("\n I is %lu and Z is %lu \n", i, z);
            if ((num % i) == 0)
                return 0;
            if (i > (num / i))
            {
                if (IsPrime(i))
                return 1;
            }
            if (z == 0)  // 0 1 0 1 0 1 0 1
            {
                i += 2;
                z = 1;
            }
            else
            {
                i += 4;
                z = 0;
            }
        }
        //  printf("\n Inside Prime Function...Number %lu is Prime \n", num);
        return 1;
}
/*****************************************************/
void main()
{
        long unsigned number, temp;
        int ret;

        printf("\n ENTER A NUMBER \n");
```

```
    scanf("%lu", &number);
    temp = number;


    do
    {
            number++;
            ret = IsPrime(number);
    }
    while (! ret);


    printf("\n SMALLEST PRIME GREATER THAN GIVEN NUMBER %lu IS %lu
\n", temp, number);
}
/**************************************************/
```

There are many steps in this program:

(a) The main function accepts the user input and calls the IsPrime function iteratively to pass the incremented numbers one by one.

(b) The IsPrime function tests the divisibility by 2, 3, and 5 and returns a negative output if the test is passed. In this manner a lot of numbers are eliminated.

(c) For testing other numbers through the sieve of Eratosthenes, it increments divisors alternately by 2 and 4. In this manner, it eliminates all the divisors that are multiples of 2 and 3. This increases the performance by a big margin as the number of operations is reduced by 64 percent (50 + 30 – 16 = 64) by this step itself.

(d) Another very important check is the comparison between divisor and quotient. If the quotient becomes smaller than divisor, that confirms the prime nature of the number. But the catch here is that such a divisor should be a prime number itself. This is being tested in my program in real time through a recursive call to the IsPrime function with the divisor as the argument.

It is through a combination of the above steps that my program works fast.

Interviewer: That is simply superb!

Ravi: Thanks, Sir. Shall I continue with my explanation?

Interviewer: Please do.

Ravi: Sir, another problem given was to simulate the square root function for finding roots of proper square numbers, again optimized for performance.

It was something that we generally don't implement. I was aware of the successive approximation method in which if we start squaring numbers from 1 onward, we can definitely find the correct square root. But that could have been very bad in performance. So the best way was to make an initial guess and then start from there. We can keep on making such guesses within number ranges to quickly eliminate many operations, but given the maximum time of 5 minutes, I could only give the logic for first guess.

This guess was based on a relationship between the number of digits in a number and the number of digits in its squared value. If you see, 9 is the largest single-digit number and 10 is the smallest two-digit number. 9's square is 81 which is of two digits and 10's square is 100 which is the smallest three-digit number. 30's square is 900, while 40's square is 1600. 100's square is 10,000, which is the smallest five-digit number. Thus, we can generalize that when the count of digits is even, the square root will be a number with half of the digits. And when the count of digits is odd, the square root would be a number with digit count equal to half plus 1. Based on this logic, I selected my starting guess as a smallest or highest half-digit number and started upward or downward from it. I am writing the same code here with a few comments.

(*While Ravi is writing, the pleased interviewer to himself: His code is very much like him, simple, yet very powerful. And look at his attitude man, damn good and a complete taskmaster attitude! He doesn't seem to mind writing it all over again for me. He is the guy who can take up a task and ensure its quickest and best completion. He has to be in my team and I will leave no stone unturned to ensure that it happens. He is the absolute FuzzySoft material. Thank God, for giving me this opportunity to talk to such a gem of a student.*)

```
/*****************************************************/
#include <stdio.h>
```

```
void main()
{
        float number, num, inter = 1, guess = 0;
        int i, j;

        printf("\n Supply a proper square number");
        scanf("%f", &number);

        num = number;

/*****************************************************/
// Count number of digits

        for (i=1; ;i++)
        {       num = num / 10;
                if (num < 10)
                {       i++;
                        printf("\n Number of digits in %f is : %d \n", number, i);
                        break;
                        }
        }
/*****************************************************/
// Make the first guess to start approximation

        for (j=1;(j <= (i / 2)) ;j++ )
        {               inter = inter * 10;                }
        printf("\n Intermediate guess is : %f \n", inter);
/*****************************************************/
// Skip if first guess is right :)

        if ((inter * inter) == number);

/*****************************************************/
// If it is an odd digit number, the square root would be more than the initial
guess
```

```
        else
        {       if (i % 2)
                {       do
                        {               inter++;
                                        guess = inter * inter;
                                        //printf("\n Intermediate is : %d and guess is : %d \n",
inter, guess);
                        }
                        while (guess < number);
                }
                /*******************************************************/
// If it is an even digit number, the square root would be less than the initial
guess
                else
                {       do
                        {               inter--;
                                        guess = inter * inter;
                                        //printf("\n Intermediate is : %d and guess is : %d \n",
inter, guess);
                        }
                        while (guess > number);
                }
        }
/*******************************************************/
        printf("\n square root of %f is %f \n", number, inter);
}
/*******************************************************/
```

Interviewer (*smiling*): That was pretty neat! I liked the concept of this programming contest. Unusual, but it checks a programmer's basics under intense pressure. And I am extremely happy to see you could execute the interesting logic through the beautiful programs!

Ravi (*grateful at compliments being showered on him*): Thank you, Sir, thank you very much for your appreciation. I am happy that I could explain my thoughts to you.

Interviewer (*smiling*): The pleasure is all mine, Ravi! Let's talk about computer fundamentals a little bit. Tell me something about computer memory.

Ravi: Sir, there are many levels of memory in a computer which are accessed hierarchically. The memory built right next to the ALU of a processor is the register memory. Then there are different types of cache memories, followed by the RAM, the main memory. Next is the virtual memory, after which come the hard disk or secondary storage and external drives like the tape drives to form the last level. I will explain the functioning through a diagram.

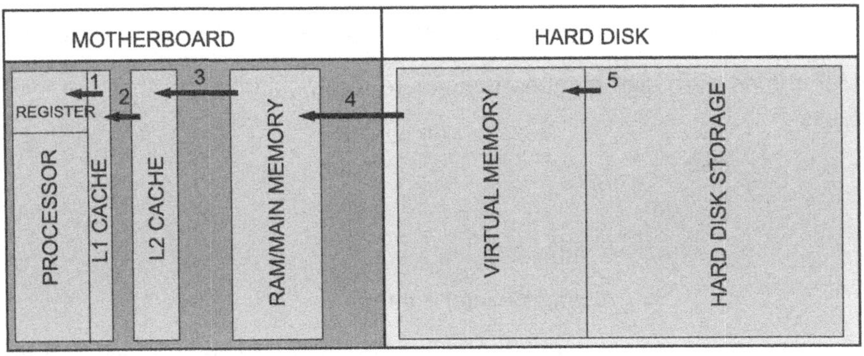

Ravi (*confidently*): Sir, the most frequently accessed data or the data that is being operated upon right now by the processor is stored in the registers. Technically, registers are the expensive memory cells built in the ALU and they can be directly accessed by the processor. They work at almost the same speed as the CPU. Level 1 cache is a type of static RAM which is also built on the processor chip. It speeds up the performance by the concept of the locality of reference, which assumes that chunks of program needed by the processor at any point of time are stored at consecutive locations; hence they can be cached on a location closest to the processor.

L2 cache is the memory bank located on the motherboard, right next to the CPU, and it can be accessed at the speed of the system bus. Cache memory is generally small in size of few megabytes but greatly improves the performance. RAM is the next level of memory. If some data is not found in the L2 cache, it is searched inside the RAM. All the active programs are loaded in the RAM. Some systems have an L3 cache also, in which case L1 and L2 caches are built on the CPU chip itself and L3 is embedded onto the motherboard.

To explain virtual memory, let's take an example. We have a 1 GB RAM and there are 10 programs to be loaded, each with a size of 200 MB, that is a total size of 2 GB. This situation is handled by the concept of virtual memory. It is a section of the hard disk that is used to store open, yet inactive programs code and serve as a backup for the RAM. In this example, the five last accessed programs' code will be moved over to the virtual memory area. Operating systems allow soft control on the virtual memory size and users can set it to various sizes like 1 GB, 2 GB, 4 GB, etc. Paging concept is involved in the virtual memory usage.

If the virtual memory minimum size specified is 512 MB and the maximum size specified is 2 GB, RAM size is 1 GB, then swapping data between RAM and virtual memory would involve four pages of 512 MB each. A page forms a part of the RAM content that is exchanged between the RAM and the hard disk.

Hard disk is the permanent storage area, which is magnetic in nature. Data access time is very high for this level of memory. Whenever there is a data request, data from hard disk is copied onto the RAM from where it is accessed by the processor.

Interviewer: What is the difference between pen drive, RAM, and hard disk memory types?

Ravi: Sir, RAM is a chip-based memory, which uses CMOS transistors to store data. As the output of these transistors dies in the absence of power, RAM cannot be used for permanent data storage. This design gives RAM its capability to be accessed randomly and quickly through the system bus based on the address values.

Hard disk is magnetic memory. It consists of multiple magnetic disks mounted on a spindle and read and written by a magnetic head. The head is positioned and the spindle is rotated to read or write data.

Pen drives use a type of electrically erasable and programmable ROM. The individual memory units are built by the MOSFET gates. A gate is kept insulated from the rest of the circuit, but it can be charged by depositing an electron on it when it is powered on. This is the writing process. After power is removed, this electron cannot escape because of insulation. This electron thus stores the bit. A combination of many such gates on a chip makes the memory element of a pen drive.

Interviewer: Can you draw the circuit of this MOSFET?

Ravi: Sorry Sir, I am not very comfortable with the electronics of circuit design. I took the help of a few electronics friends to get a basic understanding of the transistor functioning, but I cannot draw the circuits or do the voltage or current calculations for a given transistor-based circuit, and certainly not for MOSFETs.

Interviewer (*smiling*): You are a CS student and I can understand that. Circuits scare even Electronics students! As a CS student, what is your view on social networking sites?

Ravi (*excited*): Sir, they are all about very smart algorithms and programming. Algorithm that can maintain input relationships, and based on those inputs, discover further connections. Algorithm that is intelligent enough to keep track of changes and convey those changes to all the connections that matter in shortest possible time. And given the popularity of Facebook, it is about a lot of investment also, in terms of storage space and continuously running the application under such a heavy load. I am not a party to their proprietary algorithms, but it must be a lot about dynamic html for the front-end which interacts with a very robust back-end database. And all this interaction is supported by many sub-algorithms for making the system very fast and keeping it always up and running. I can draw an analogy between a site like Facebook and a computer system itself. The algorithm is the processor which keeps track of the system processes and these system processes are nothing but the activities of the millions of users online. I am sure they must have identical copies of their servers located across many continents, so that users across the globe can access the application at almost the same speed.

And last but not the least, social networking is about money. It needs to be backed up by a robust revenue generating model that can sustain this system and earn some money for its creators.

(*Delighted Interviewer to himself: That's really cool talk! I am not telling you this, but believe me, I have asked many students the same question, and as a reply, most of them compared the existing sites like LinkedIn, Facebook, Orkut, etc., based on their features. A couple of them did speak about Zuckerberg developing a program as a part of his project to connect people and the project becoming an instant hit, but nothing as complete as yours! Essentially, they spoke from a user's perspective and you spoke from a developer's perspective and I liked that immensely. Boy, if that is not an exaggeration, I see another Larry Page in you! Let me grill you just a little more before I let you go.*)

Interviewer: Ravi, that was an interesting viewpoint! Now can you please help me understand the difference between 32-bit and 64-bit systems?

Ravi: Sure, Sir. 32-bit and 64-bit systems comprise of a processor and address bus system which can work in either of these two modes and all the software that is installed on top of it. We can start from the processor. A 32-bit processor has registers with a 32-bit word capacity, which means that a single word of maximum 32 bits can be stored in the register. Now memory addresses are also stored in registers before they can be given to the address bus. So an address bus connected to a 32-bit register would be of 32-bit size generally. 32-bit width translates to a maximum value of 4 GB, that is, it can uniquely identify up to approximately 4 billion addresses and not beyond. This limits the maximum RAM size that can be used with a 32-bit processor to 4 GB. A single bus is multiplexed as data and address bus depending upon the read or write signal from the processor. This limits data width to 32 bits also. So if there is 40-bit-wide data to be operated upon, the processor will first operate upon the lower 32 bits, then discard them and use the next 8 bits. This makes processing slower.

Given this limitation and recent advances in memory technology, 64-bit systems have become commonplace. Such processors have 64-bit-wide registers to directly handle 64-bit-wide data. Also, the addressing capability of a 64-bit bus is huge; I don't remember the exact number but it is 2 to the power 64, which looks way beyond our current memory capabilities.

Interviewer: You must have read about adder and subtractor circuits. Haven't you?

Ravi: Yes, Sir, I have.

Interviewer (*curious*): Have you also read about multiplier and divider circuits?

Ravi: No, Sir.

Interviewer: Why so, Ravi?

Ravi: Sir, binary multiplication and division operations are much simpler than thought. A multiplication or division can be implemented through a series of shift and add operations. There might be many types of implementations, but a shift operation is at the heart of multiplication and division. And we did study about shift registers.

Interviewer: All right, Ravi! It was a pleasure talking to you. I hope to see you at FuzzySoft office within few months. I see it's celebrations time for you right now! Good-bye.

Ravi: Thank you, Sir!

SCENE 3

The interviewer proudly looks at Ravi as he is leaving the room. He starts filling Ravi's evaluation sheet enthusiastically. Technical breadth and depth are marked excellent with a comment, "Well read and aware; Understands computer basics very well." Programming skills are marked exceptional with a comment, "Basic, performance oriented, innovative and smart." Communication is rated excellent with a comment, "Communicates better than professionals." The "Any other comments" section is scribbled with these words: "Exceptionally brilliant and focused. Cannot be treated at par with other campus recruits. Should be assigned to one of our latest research project teams that will offer him challenges suited to his capabilities."

SCENE 4

The very night, the interviewer writes a mail to his friend and colleague, the FuzzySoft campus manager.

Hey Rohit,

I am asking you for a huge personal favor though I know you have been pretty busy coordinating campus events these months. I met a whizz kid, Ravi, at CIT today. You should plan his on-boarding in a manner that he gets assigned to my team. It's a request. When you get some time, please read further to know why I am so keen to get him.

He is a saint when it comes to attitude but dresses quite well. He is a Brit when he speaks even though he has spent most of his life at a remote Indian town. His thinking faculties are highly evolved, well suited for a research team. I'll tell you his views on social networking when we meet. And he is a pro at computers. Writes such simple, powerful code; I have preserved his solution sheets for my classroom trainings! And he is a good entertainer, too – plays music, writes stories – a complete all-rounder personality. I think, given his capabilities, he would not feel very happy if assigned to a less demanding project. (Don't think this one was a marketing line!) And, of course, we do struggle to find such evolved gray cell owners, so why not pick one when luck favors.

❊ ❊ ❊

3

Electronics' Meenal at Pinnacle Computers

SCENE 1

A smartly dressed and radiant Meenal is surrounded by her equally radiant friends and they are laughing over a shared joke. Just then her name is called over for the technical round of Pinnacle Computer Technologies. She is wished good luck by her friends, who understand that she does not need it though.

SCENE 2

Interviewer: Good morning, Meenal. How are you doing?

Meenal (*warmly*): Very good morning, Sir. I am doing good, thanks.

Interviewer: Good. Please introduce yourself, Meenal.

Meenal (*enthusiastic*): Sir, I am Meenal Saxena and I am pursuing Bachelors in Technology in Electronics and Communication from the Copernicus Institute of Technology. CIT is a deemed university. I have got 7.9 CGPA till the seventh semester. My parents are doctors and I have an elder brother who is pursuing MBA. I am the associate editor of our college magazine, *Kshanika*. My hobbies are reading novels, listening to music, and playing guitar.

(Meenal: This interviewer does not appear to be smart; my goodness, such people also work for PCT! I hope to be put up with more refined folks.)

(Interviewer: This girl presents a pretty picture and her communication skills are good. Her marks are good as well, so I assume she must be good technically. Hope to wrap up this one up quickly.)

Interviewer: So, what are your four most favorite subjects?

(*Meenal: Let me name the core subjects so that he does not ask me much there.*)

Meenal: Digital electronics, communication, hmm... signal processing, and C programming.

Interviewer (*looking at her CV*): I see you have done an interesting project. Please tell me more about it.

Meenal (*confident*): Sir, we have made an elevator system that is an inexpensive replica of the usual elevator systems. In this, we have multiple modules. First was the user input module to accept the floor numbers and directions through input keys. This module interacts with the central module, which is microcontroller based. Another module was the motor drive system that moves the elevator box up and down. The power supply module supplies power to all the modules. The complete system looks like this:

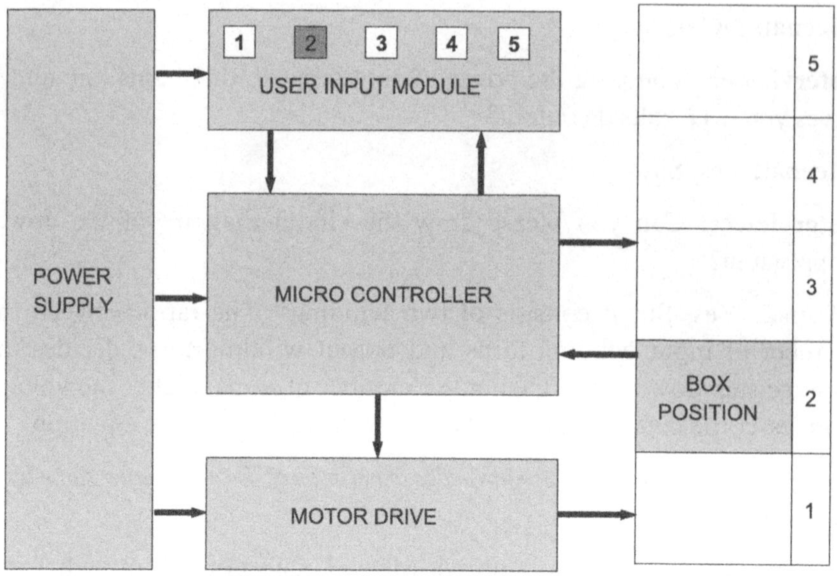

In this system, the user input is accepted by the microcontroller, which drives the motor assembly. The elevator module box is positioned at the correct floor level based on this.

Interviewer: Which microcontroller have you used?

Meenal (*unconvincing*): Sirrr ... it is 8085.

Interviewer: How did you program it? Which kit did you use? And how did you interface the motor drive to it?

Meenal (upset): Hmm ... I was, I was not in the controller or motor module.

Interviewer (curious): How was the input module constructed?

Meenal: Sorry Sir, I am not sure of that ... I was in the power supply module.

Interviewer: OK, what have you done in that?

Meenal: I have made a transformer to step down the supply voltage to 12 volts. Interviewer: Why 12 volts? 8085 works at which voltage? Can you drive a motor at such a low voltage?

Meenal: Yes Sir, it must be working at that voltage. Our guide provided us with that value.

Interviewer: I see. This 12 volts was AC or DC power?

Meenal: DC power.

Interviewer: You plug the power supply input in the mains line and it gives you a 12 volts dc output?

Meenal: Yes, Sir.

Interviewer: Can you please draw the circuit diagram of the power supply unit?

Meenal: Yes, Sir, it consists of two windings. The ratio between the number of input winding turns and output winding turns decides the voltage step down ratio. Higher the number of turns, higher the voltage and lesser the current, and vice versa. I will write down the equation.

(Interviewer: She has pathetic knowledge of her project. Let me ask her some basic questions.)

Interviewer: That is not required, Meenal. Can you tell me what is a rectifier?

Meenal: A rectifier is a circuit used to convert AC signal to DC signal. It consists of a diode that conducts in only one direction but not the other.

Interviewer: Ok Meenal, I have drawn two simple waveforms A and B. You have to tell me how we can derive the wave of Fig. B from Fig. A.

Fig. A

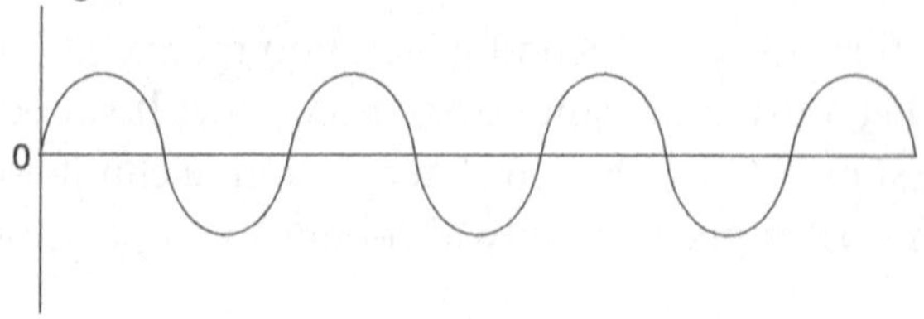

Fig. B

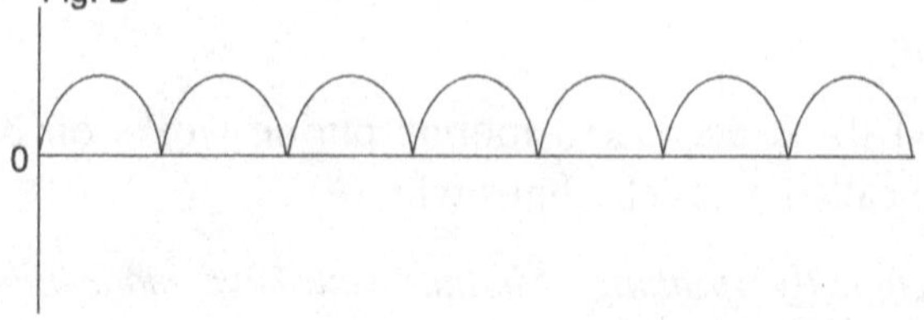

Meenal: Not sure Sir.

Interviewer: Ok, first tell me their types. I mean whether they are AC or DC and why?

Meenal: Figure A is AC wave. Figure B is hmm … it is DC … hmm … no I think it is AC.

Interviewer: How can you say that?

Meenal: Figure A is like a sine wave and AC signal is sinusoidal. Hence it is AC. DC is a constant current, it is represented by a straight line which figure B is not. So even that has to be AC.

(*Interviewer: Excellent explanation! Poor girl, you don't even know that waveform A is AC because its polarity is changing constantly. B is DC as it has no component with reversed polarity. If you feed signal A to a simple diode rectifier that you had just explained, you will get the signal waveform B. You know a transformer design and formulae by heart but don't even know it cannot be used with DC. I wonder how you have managed to score good marks with just a theoretical knowledge, as you have displayed till now.*)

Interviewer: Can you explain the threshold voltage of a diode?

Meenal (*fluently*): Sir, a diode consists of a p-n junction. P region is rich in holes and N region is rich in electrons. At the junction these holes and electrons recombine and form a depletion region and a voltage is developed across this region. A threshold voltage is required to overcome this depletion region voltage.

Interviewer: Do you know what is 2G and 3G?

Meenal: Yes, Sir. 2G is the second-generation mobile phone technology that we have been using for quite some time now. It supports voice and data transmission. 3G is the third-generation technology that works at high speed and supports bandwidth-intensive operations like video telephony.

Interviewer: Hmm ... Do you know why the mobile phone is also called as a cell phone?

Meenal: Sir, I think because a mobile phone works on battery, and a battery is also called as a cell, that's why.

(*Interviewer: Honestly speaking, Meenal, you have made my day by your entertaining replies. I cannot select you, but will remember you for many days to come.*)

Interviewer: Do you have a laptop?

Meenal: Yes, Sir.

Interviewer: Which brand?

Meenal: Lenovo.

Interviewer: It has a fingerprint-based locking system, right?

Meenal: Yes, Sir.

Interviewer: Signal processing is your favorite subject, right? Tell me how does the fingerprint recognition system work?

Meenal: Sir, it registers the fingerprint first. Then in future, it tries to match the input fingerprint against the one stored in the database.

Interviewer: Yup! How does it try to match the two fingerprints?

Meenal (*smiling sheepishly*): Hmm ... not sure.

Interviewer (*smiling*): How does a fingerprint scanner work, do you have any idea on that?

Meenal (*still smiling sheepishly*): Hmm ... no Sir.

Interviewer (*smiling*): Hmm ... no worries. Let's talk about your hobby, listening to music. Do you listen to FM?

Meenal (*smiling*): Yes, Sir.

Interviewer: Which is your favorite station?

Meenal: Many stations. Radio Mirchi works the best for me as it offers a wide variety of retro classics.

Interviewer: What does FM stand for?

Meenal (*grim*): Frequency modulation.

Interviewer: What is AM?

Meenal: Amplitude modulation.

Interviewer: No, I mean what is amplitude modulation?

Meenal: In amplitude modulation, the amplitude of the carrier signal is varied in accordance with the message signal. The carrier signal has a much higher frequency than the message signal.

Interviewer (*smiling*): Good; why do you see FM stations all around and no AM stations?

Meenal (*guessing*): Hmm … maybe because of quality. FM's quality is better than AM.

Interviewer: Hmm … how can you say so?

Meenal (*giving up*): I don't know, Sir!

Interviewer: No worries, Meenal! Tell me something technical that you know and understand very well.

Meenal (*thinking*): Sir, we studied digital electronics and I found it very interesting. I know the gates like OR, AND, NAND, etc. I liked the concept of multiplexers, coders, decoders, adders, etc. Shall I draw a full adder circuit?

Interviewer: Please do.

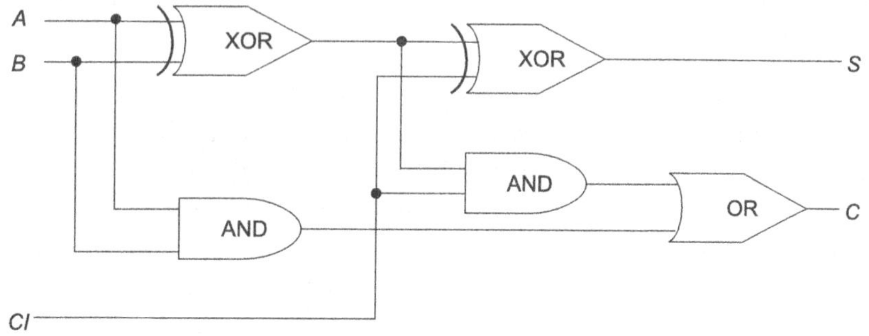

Meenal (*enthusiastic*): In this circuit, A and B are the two bits to be added and CI is is the input carry from any other previous operation. A and B are XORed and then the output is XORed with CI to generate the sum bit. Output Carry C is generated by ANDing the inputs and ANDing the input carry with the XORed inputs. This is finally fed to the OR gate to generate C.

(Interviewer: Fine then, I should let this parrot go at this not so sad juncture.)

Interviewer: Very good, Meenal. I have no more questions. You may leave now.

Meenal: Thank you, Sir. Good day, Sir!

SCENE 3

Meenal has come out of the ordeal and does not look very comfortable. She tells her friends that she is confused about the outcome as she could answer half of the questions very well and half of them did not go well.

The interviewer is upset as he thinks Meenal has no engineering aptitude. He thinks that some of his friends might have selected her for her theoretical know-how, fine talking, and smart dressing, but he is certainly not one of them. He quickly fills her form with a Tech Reject decision. Technical skills are evaluated as poor with remarks "theoretical ok, practical very poor." He additionally writes a general remark, "Completely lacks aptitude."

SCENE 4

Hello my netizen friends, wondering where I had been for the last fortnight? I was talking to students with the purpose of recruiting some of them. It was a nice experience as usual with a lot of fun and a little of dilemma. Let me narrate the tragically funny story of Miss M, whom I met this time.

Miss M is a fine-talking lady; she can even read technical books and memorize the content like a story book. She is good at theory if you ask her direct questions. You can ask her what is a DC or AC wave and I am sure you will get the best reply from the best book that even I cannot provide. Trust me, I was reminded of the 3 Idiots' "fan definition" scene. But don't throw a random wave at her and ask her about its type!

I know some people can recruit her – she talks well, is smart, answers questions well – but honestly speaking, I felt that she has wasted an engineering seat. I know from experience that she must have cried a lot on learning about her rejection because people of her type are generally not rejected. This thought was weighing heavily on my conscience but I cannot go by mere face value. Her conceptual level is at absolute zero. Don't know why FM, not AM, stations are in vogue, how fingerprint scanners work; yet she can read out entire communication and signal processing books to you even without looking at the book!

Listing such subjects as favorites must have been a calculated move on her part, which obviously backfired. These days students are getting smarter and believe that IT folks would remember nothing from their own college days. They forget that we had to study really hard to get a job in those days!

And the icing on the fun cake was my learning of the wonderful reason why mobile phones are called cell phones. After all they run on battery and battery is synonymous to a cell! ☺

Waiting for your verdict on my verdict on Miss M …

⁂ ⁂ ⁂

4

IT's Puneet Goes for Apogee Informatics

SCENE 1

Tensed Puneet is being encouraged by his friends and he is still feeling the butterflies in his stomach. He complains of a parched throat and is offered Coke, which he gulps down quickly. He is cursing his luck for being made to wait for long for his turn. In the heart of his heart, he is confident about his knowledge but this wait and the glum faces all around are killing him. One of his friends wittily drifts the discussion toward cricket and the next fifteen minutes pass without agonizing him.

SCENE 2

Puneet: Good evening, Sir! I am Puneet.

Interviewer: Good evening, Puneet. Take a seat please. You look tired.

Puneet (*nervous*): It has been a long and hot day, Sir, maybe because of that. But I am not feeling tired at all.

(The Interviewer makes out his nervousness and tries to calm him down by some casual talk.)

Interviewer: That's good to know. Tell me how you generally spend weekends.

Puneet (*smiling*): Sir, half of the weekend is lost in sleeping till late. Then the remaining part of the day is generally spent in exploring the city and the places around. Sometimes we watch movies back to back.

Interviewer (*mischievously*): Where does a girlfriend fit in this schedule?

Puneet (*smiling*): I haven't been lucky till now, Sir! Anyhow, I do enjoy this freedom where we set out on long bike rides in the evening and do not return before dawn.

Interviewer (*smiling*): Hmm ... you are reminding me of my good old college days and making me jealous. Can I see your resume please? I haven't got my copy.

Puneet: Sure, Sir.

(*Browsing through the resume, the interviewer comes across many references to C language and he writes few lines on a paper and asks Puneet for the output.*)

Puneet: Sir, the first statement

int x[10] = {1,2,3,4,5,6,7,8,9,10,11,12};

will give compilation error as more elements are included than defined in the size of the array. So we will have to strike out the last two values from the list.

1. int x[10] = {1,2,3,4,5,6,7,8,9,10~~,11,12~~};

The second statement is syntactically valid but logically incorrect.

2. x[10] = 13;

We are trying to assign value to an address that falls outside the addresses kept aside for the array x. As C does not support inherent bound checking, the value 13 will be written to any location depending upon the starting element address. If that location is empty, that will be fine, but if there is any meaningful data there, it will be silently overwritten, which is dangerous. It is actually a virus code.☺

I will write the results as comments for all the other statements.

3. int x[10] = {}; // Error – Blank initialization not possible
4. int x[10] = {0}; // All values assigned 0
5. int x[] = {1,2,3,4}; // Array x of size 4 created
6. int x[]; / / Error, either values or size required
7. int x[] = {1,2, , 4, , 6, , , 9, 10}; // Error , missing values not allowed

Interviewer: How can you swap the following variables without using a third variable?

Initial values:

X = 'A', Y = 'B'

Final values:

X = 'B', Y = 'A'

Puneet: Sir, we can use the same trick as applied for swapping numbers.

```
/*************************************************************/
        char X = 'A', Y = 'B';
        printf("\n X is %c Y is %c \n", X, Y);
        X = X + Y;
        Y = X - Y;
        X = X - Y;
        printf("\n X is %c Y is %c \n", X, Y);
/*************************************************************/
```

Interviewer: What would be the ouput for the following lines?

```
/*************************************************************/
#include <stdio.h>
void main()
{
struct a{
char name[5];    // Name
int age;         // Age in years
float sal;    // Salary in thousands
};
struct a emp = {'j', 'k', 'l', 35, 69.5};
printf("\n %c, %d, %f \n", emp.name[4], emp.age, emp.sal);
}
/*************************************************************/
```

Puneet: We are assigning values to the structure emp elements. Is a missing pair of braces going to throw an error … hmm … I don't think so. In that case it should assign all values to the name array. How about 69.5 … that will be truncated, I guess. Sir, the ouput should be "E, 0, 0.0000."

(Interviewer: That's good, you do understand the language basics!)

Interviewer (*smiling*): How did you arrive at that?

Puneet: Since the first element of the structure is an array of length 5 and the initialization set consists of five values only, all of them get assigned to the array 'name' and the other next elements of the structure get initialized with data type defaults.

Within the character array "name," 35 and 69 are considered as ASCII codes and their respective characters are assigned at fourth and fifth positions. I am not sure about the character for ASCII code 35; for 69, it is "E."

The next two elements, age and salary, are initialized to data type defaults.

Interviewer: Explain inheritance.

Puneet: Sir, it is a feature supported by object-oriented programming languages like C++ and Java. It allows creating hierarchical code. I will explain it through one example.

Undergraduate students form a class that exhibits certain common features like enjoying freedom from school for the first time, trying to study beyond a list of prescribed books, preparing for jobs, etc.

Engineering students form a sub-class of the general class of UG students. They display the above features and have certain specific traits like being louder, experimenting more with technology by creating robots and other working models, etc.

IT students form a more specialized class where they are expected to go more into the web technologies and so on.

Back to Java, a top-level class or a super-class is constructed. Next a more specific sub-class is constructed with only the specific features defined. All the generic features get inherited from the super-class. In the definition of the sub-class, 'extends' keyword needs to be used.

A sub-class can become a super-class for a further sub-class and so on. I will draw a quick diagram also which makes it look more like a Venn diagram and best explains inheritance.

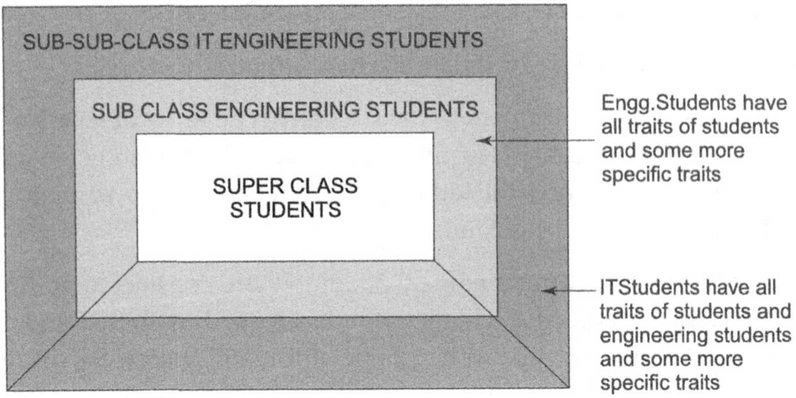


```
class Students{ }
class EnggStudents extends Students { }
class ITStudents extends EnggStudents { }
```

Interviewer: The Venn diagram analogy is cool!

Puneet: Thanks Sir. It has helped me understand classes in the right perspective. Otherwise a word like super-class sometimes confuses us into believing that the sub classes would be sub-sets when, in reality, the relationship is just the opposite.

Interviewer: That's interesting.

(One of the other panelists, who has been an alumnus, walks into the room and asks Puneet, "Is he troubling you much? Let me know if he is." Puneet replies, "Not at all Sir, I am enjoying the discussion." On hearing this, the alumnus leaves the room, smiling.)

Interviewer (*teasing*): Was that an honest reply, Puneet?

Puneet (*smiling*): Yes Sir, of course. Frankly, I was a bit tensed waiting for my turn, but I feel comfortable now. Thanks for putting me at ease.

Interviewer (*smiling*): Good to know that! I can see from your resume that you have done html coding for your college website. I happen to carry a simple printout. Please take a few minutes of your time to look at it and write the code for it. Here it is:

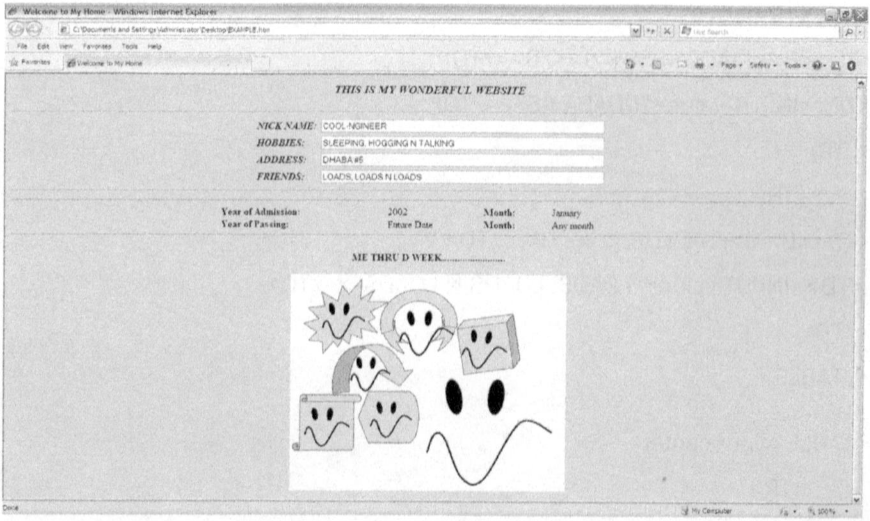

(Puneet smiles at the printout, analyzes it, jots down the main sections, and ends up writing almost correct code.)

```
/****************************************************************/
<html>
	<head>
		<title>Welcome to My Home</title>
	</head>

	<body BGCOLOR="#888888">
	<P align=center><B><I>THIS IS MY WONDERFUL WEBSITE</I></B></P>

<TABLE align=center>
<TR>
<TD><B><I>NICK NAME:</I></B></TD>
<TD><INPUT value="COOL-NGINEER"></TD>
</TR>
	<TR>
<TD><B><I>HOBBIES:</I></B></TD>
<TD><INPUT value="SLEEPING, HOGGING N TALKING"></TD>
</TR>
```

```
        <TR>
<TD><B><I>ADDRESS:</I></B></TD>
<TD><INPUT value="DHABA #5"></TD>
</TR>
        <TR>
<TD><B><I>FRIENDS:</I></B></TD>
 <TD><INPUT value="LOADS, LOADS N LOADS"></TD>
</TR>
</TABLE>

<TABLE align=center>
        <TR>
<TD><B>Year of Admission:</B></TD>
<TD> 2002 </TD>
<TD><B>Month: </B></TD>
<TD>January</TD>
</TR>
        <TR>
<TD><B>Year of Passing:</B></TD>
<TD> Future Date </TD>
<TD><B>Month: </B></TD>
<TD> Any month</TD>
</TR>
</TABLE>

<TABLE>
<TR>
<TD>ME THRU D WEEK..........................</TD>
<TD><img src="C:\image.jpg" /></TD>
        </TR>
</TABLE>
</body>
</html>
/*************************************************************/
```

Interviewer: Can you please explain all the tags that you have used?

Puneet: Yes, Sir.

1. html tag specifies the language used.
2. title tag determines the value for the title bar.

3. body BGCOLOR determines the page background color. I have used hexadecimal values 888888, which will generate a shade of gray as all the three components RGB are in equal measure.
4. Then I create a table with table tag and specify rows with TR (table row) and columns with TD (table data) tag.
5. img tag is used to display images. src specifies the image location, where I have put a hypothetical value.

Interviewer: That's perfect! As you have worked with database also, can you write SQL?

Puneet: Sir, we have used Oracle and SQL Server for our back-end for our project. I can write basic SQL.

Interviewer: OK, here I draw this table.

Customer_Purchase

Customer_Id	Name	Product	Quantity	Unit_Price
4	RAHUL	CHIPS SALTED	2	20
6	SIM	CHIPS TANGY	1	25
1	ADITYA	CHOCOLATES	3	50
4	RAHUL	CAKE	1	30
1	ADITYA	COLD DRINK	4	20
2	POOJA	COOKIES	5	10
2	POOJA	CHOCOLATES	1	50
2	POOJA	CHIPS SALTED	4	20

Interviewer: Please write the SQL for creating this table (First column cannot contain nulls).

Puneet: I will write the Create Table statement for this:

```
CREATE TABLE CUSTOMER_PURCHASE
(CUSTOMER_ID VARCHAR2(5) NOT NULL,
```

```
NAME VARCHAR2(25),
PRODUCT VARCHAR2(25),
QUANTITY NUMBER,
UNIT_PRICE NUMBER);
```

Interviewer: Why did you make Customer Id as varchar?

Puneet: Sir, ID fields might be alphanumeric. Our student ids also are combination of numbers and alphabets.

Interviewer: Hmm ... How can I see all the records from this table?

Puneet: By select statement: SELECT * FROM CUSTOMER_PURCHASE;

Interviewer: Suppose this table is empty and you have to write the first record into it; how will you do that?

Puneet: Many times we use the SQL Server GUI to do this, but we can also use insert statement:

```
INSERT INTO CUSTOMER_PURCHASE
(CUSTOMER_ID, NAME, PRODUCT, QUANTITY, UNIT_PRICE)
VALUES
('4', 'RAHUL', 'CHIPS SALTED', 2, 20);

COMMIT;
```

Interviewer: Why do you specify column names and what is that Commit?

Puneet: Sir, if we have to insert values for few columns, then we need to specify a list, otherwise not. But in our project, we had not specified a list initially. Then later, our guide suggested some changes and we had to expand the table. That time we had to rewrite all the statements as the front-end was still sending values for the initial list of columns only.

Commit is to save it. It is like the save button. Data goes from RAM to hard disk.

Interviewer: How can I find how many unique customers are there in this table?

Puneet: Hmm ... we will use count for that.

```
SELECT COUNT(DISTINCT CUSTOMER_ID) AS CUSTOMER FROM CUSTOMER_
PURCHASE;
```

Interviewer: Write SQL to find the total quantities sold for each product. Your output should look like this:

```
      SUM PRODUCT
----------------------------
        6 CHIPS SALTED
        5 COOKIES
        4 COLD DRINK
        4 CHOCOLATES
        1 CAKE
        1 CHIPS TANGY
6 rows selected.
```

Puneet: I will use Group By function.

```
SELECT SUM(QUANTITY) AS SUM, PRODUCT FROM CUSTOMER_PURCHASE
GROUP BY PRODUCT ORDER BY SUM DESC;
```

(As Puneet completes writing the statement, a volunteer serves wafers, biscuits, and tea.)

Interviewer: See, what a coincidence, Puneet, I made you hungry counting goodies and here we are served some. Please help yourself. It is a treat for your knowledge. ☺

(Puneet thanks the interviewer but is hesitant to accept the offer. When the interviewer insists, he joins him and they talk about the city munching on the goodies.)

Interviewer: You have mentioned networks as your favorite subject and also worked for the college site. Help me understand a simple URL structure like this:

http://www.yourcollege.ac.in/fest2010/contest.htm

Puneet: This address has many parts. 'http' is the first part, it means the protocol to access is the http protocol. 'www' means it is on the World Wide Web domain, inside that in the India academic domain, 'in' is for India and 'ac' for academic.

yourcollege is the website name, technically it is the name of the hosting machine.

fest2010 is the path on the machine like we have C drive, D drive etc.

contest.htm is the code file in the fest2010 path and it has the code to display the page content. So the broken parts look like this:

http://www.yourcollege.ac.in/fest2010/contest.htm

Interviewer: Excellent; do you know why am I asking related questions instead of directly asking you about your project?

Puneet (*suspecting a trap*): Hmm … No, Sir …

Interviewer (*smiling*): Because students have become very smart these days. They start fluently with the theoretical description of their projects and leave no scope to ask questions and we cannot determine if they have really implemented anything! And going the other way round, I can see that you have indeed written your own project code and not purchased it from a professional. ☺

Puneet (*smiling cautiously*): Yes Sir. We had initially planned to get it done from outside. But then our guide set up the Oracle database and helped us with the connectivity. Things became easier then and we could manage the project ourselves. It saved us a lot of money also. ☺

Interviewer (*smiling*): Good work, Puneet! Let's call it a day on this good note. Now it's my turn to say that I enjoyed talking to you.

Puneet: Thanks, Sir. Bye.

SCENE 3

Puneet's friends are anxiously waiting for him. They surround him and start enquiring about the ordeal. He confides that he was getting nervous unnecessarily and that the interviewer was a chilled-out man.

The interviewer marks Puneet as a Select. He adds comments, "Puneet has a good understanding of programming. He has indeed worked on his project and understands C, html, and databases well. Overall he could justify his IT studies. A straight-talking, frank, and team-spirited person; also great at explaining stuff. He has a good solid base and should be comfortable to work on any technology."

SCENE 4

The interviewer makes a detailed personal record of the reasons for selection for any future reference:

Name: Puneet Mehra, Batch: January 2011, College: RITS, Branch: IT

My Reference Point: The true web designer

Miscellaneous:

1. In sync with his branch, he knows databases quite well and has a good experience in writing SQL, a trait not generally seen in students.
2. Understands networking concepts and writes basic HTML quite fast and accurate, an experience gained through real project work.
3. Good at programming and C concepts. Very well understands Java concepts. Both of which are my minimum expectations from an IT guy.
4. A gifted instructor; conveys his thoughts in a very organized and clear fashion. I can already see his teammates queuing up at his desk for understanding project requirements and designs. And he is aware of this strength.
5. Has taken initiative for college website design and that is a good EC activity with a lot of responsibility. It would be nice to have such motivated people in your team.
6. Another good thing about him is that he talks straight and does not beat around the bush.

Weakness ... what do I jot down for that? Strange, I could not manage time to find that out, may be I should improve upon my interviewing skills in that case! Puneet, I must say you must have fared very well so that I remained focused on your strength areas and became blind to the weak areas.

❋ ❋ ❋

5

Mechanical's Siddhartha Enjoys at Intella Systems

SCENE 1

Siddhartha is jolted out of sleep by his friends who tell him that the Intella interviews are going to start an hour earlier, that is, in another 15 minutes and his name is on the top of the list. The only thought now playing upon his mind is to reach the venue in time. The tie is forgotten in the hurry-burry. Socks are not matched, and shoes are not shined. Riding pillion, he imagines a complete blackout. But he does manage to get dropped at the computer lab just as his name is called out.

SCENE 2

Siddhartha (*panting*): Hello Sir, Siddhartha wishes you a very good morning! **Interviewer (*startled by the dudish greeting*):** Good ... good morning, Siddhartha. I would call you Sid if you please so.

Siddhartha: Please do, Sir. That's how I am known here.

Interviewer (*offering a glass of water*): Looks like you have just returned from the morning jog; please take a sip!

Sid (*smiling sheepishly*): Thank you, Sir!

Sorry Sir, I had to sort of rush. I got a bit late today morning as it had got very late by the time the results were announced last night.

Interviewer (*warily*): Why, are you coordinating the event and also participating in it?

Sid: Yeah.

Interviewer: What's the need to coordinate then?

Sid: Sir, this is the first IT company for the season and it is open to all. For this reason, some of us need to coordinate this event as well.

Interviewer (*smiling*): Well said, well said! So how are the coordinators picked, through a lottery draw?

Sid (*smiling*): Not really! It's a volunteered activity.

Interviewer (*appearing distant*): I happened to see this data in the morning paper about a new car being launched.

Engine	
Fuel	Petrol
Material	All Aluminium Cylinder Engine
No. of Cylinders	4
No. of Valves	16
Valve Train Type	DOHC

Sid (*curious*): Which car it is?

Interviewer: Oh never mind the car! Just help me understand this jargon.

(Sid: Gosh, You managed to sneak in this piece of paper! How deeply you must have been thinking about interviewing us!)

Sid: Here they are talking about some of the important technical specifications of the car engine. It is an aluminium engine that runs on petrol. It has got four cylinders. An engine with more cylinders gives a smoother performance and is easier to start. Then there are four valves per cylinder. These are the intake and exhaust valves. The intake valves send the fuel into the engine cylinder and the exhaust valves drive out the gases produced during ignition. Now these valves are operated through overhead cams. Cam is the mechanism that opens and closes valves depending on the stroke the engine is going through. A cam is just the reverse of the crank mechanism. It converts rotations into vertical motion. DOHC implies dual overhead camshaft, where one cam controls the intake valves and the other controls the exhaust valves. And the …

Interviewer (*interrupting*): That was truly enlightening! How did you travel to the college today?

Sid: I rode my bike, Sir.

Interviewer: Hmm bike, that's interesting…which model?

Sid: Sir, it is Bajaj Pulsar.

Interviewer: No! No! No, tell me like a mechie!

Sid: All right, Sir! It's Bajaj Pulsar 220 DTSi.

Interviewer: What does DTSi stand for?

Sid: Dual Twin Spark-Plug Ignition.

Interviewer: What do the numbers 2, 2, and 0 represent?

Sid (*confused*): 2, 2, 0 … hmm … yeah, they are not separate numbers. It's two hundred and twenty and that's the engine cylinder displacement volume.

Interviewer: Here 220 is a single cylinder displacement or all the cylinders combined?

Sid: It is for a single cylinder here, as it is a single-cylinder engine bike. But generally, the displacement specified for any vehicle is the combined displacement of all the cylinders.

Interviewer: How do you calculate displacement?

Sid: You need to know the bore and stroke values. Bore is the cylinder diameter and stroke is the distance between the BDC and the TDC. Then displacement can be calculated as the volume of a cylinder with height equal to stroke and dia equal to the bore. That becomes

$$\pi \times \text{stroke} \times (\text{bore}/2)^2.$$

Interviewer: What is DTSi, the "Dual Twin Spark-Plug Ignition" technology?

Sid: There are two spark plugs in the combustion chamber to better ignite the fuel. One moment, Sir, it is "Digital Twin Spark", not "Dual Twin Spark." As auto electronics control the ignition timing, it is digital ignition.

Interviewer: What about the brake and tire types?

Sid: Tubeless tires and disk brake system, which is a norm now.

Interviewer (*smiling*): You have done a good homework. Were you expecting questions on your bike?

Sid (*grinning*): Yeah, sort of!

Interviewer: We don't get to see diesel bikes as frequently as diesel cars. Has it got anything to do with the better mileage of a motorcycle engine as opposed to a car engine?

Sid: Correlation with the mileage … maybe, yeah. That might be a reason why the market isn't demanding diesel bikes as much.

Interviewer: What do you think is the other reason then?

Sid: It is about the size of the engine. Motorcycles demand smaller engines and diesel engines can't be made as small as petrol engines. The diesel engine works on self-ignition, which needs a high compression ratio to increase the air temperature to a high value. Higher compression ratio requirement makes the diesel engine bulky and unsuited for bikes.

Interviewer: Would you please explain how bicycle brakes work?

Sid (*confused*): You mean the bicycle or the bike?

Interviewer: I said bicycle.

Sid: A bicycle brake system is pretty simple. You pull the brake handle; it pulls the cable which moves the brake pads upward onto the rim and holds it there.

Interviewer: What is the difference between the brakes you just explained and car brakes?

Sid: Cars rely on drum and disk brakes. Disk brakes are more commonly used these days. The basic difference in the entire brake system design between a cycle and car stems from the fact that a car would need a much higher force. So car brakes cannot be completely manual or cable based. The car brake system consists of the following components:

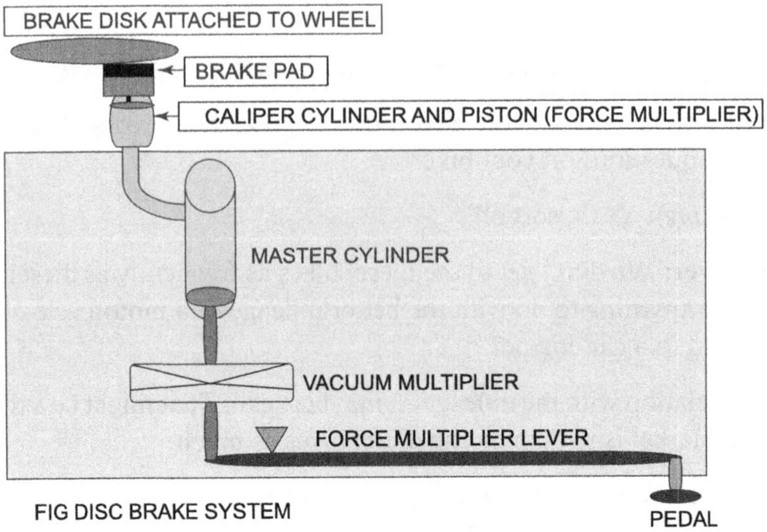

FIG DISC BRAKE SYSTEM

As you can see, the three levels of force multiplication through simple physics principles provide the enormous braking power required for stopping a car.

Another difference is the use of disk brake, which provides much higher efficiency. The brake pads press the brake disk from both sides, slowing down is rotational speed. In this diagram, I have included the brake pads on only one side of the disc. Actually, there are two brake pads; there are two brake lines coming out of the master cylinder.

(Sid: What a strange situation, I came all prepped up for an IT interview and this guy is hell-bent on analyzing my bike. How could have I remembered this much if I had not done my summer training with Eicher!)

Interviewer: Which is more powerful, a two-stroke engine or a four-stroke one?

Sid: A four-stroke engine.

Interviewer: Why do you say so? As far as I understand, every second stroke is a power stroke in a two-stroke engine!

Sid: That is correct. But a two-stroke engine cylinder cannot be sealed during the entire power stroke and that results in a huge loss of power. A four-stroke engine's intake and exhaust valves remain closed during the power stroke, which in turn results in a much higher power being delivered to the crank. And a large flywheel compensates for irregular power generated by the strokes of a four-stroke engine to an extent.

Interviewer: Please carry on!

Sid: If we look at this simplified diagram of a two-stroke engine, we can see that the intake valve opens when the compression cycle is ON. Thus intake and compression happen simultaneously. The compression ratio becomes smaller as the intake sleeve has to close first. Then, at the end of the power stroke, the exhaust valve opens. As the intake sleeve is also open at the same time, a part of fresh fuel is also lost, thereby reducing the engine efficiency and making it very polluting.

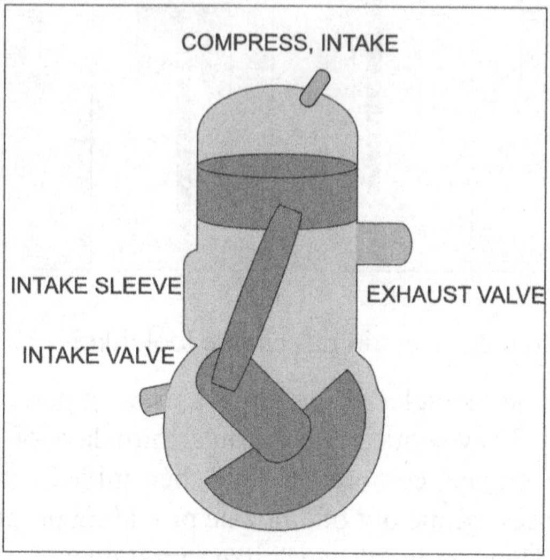

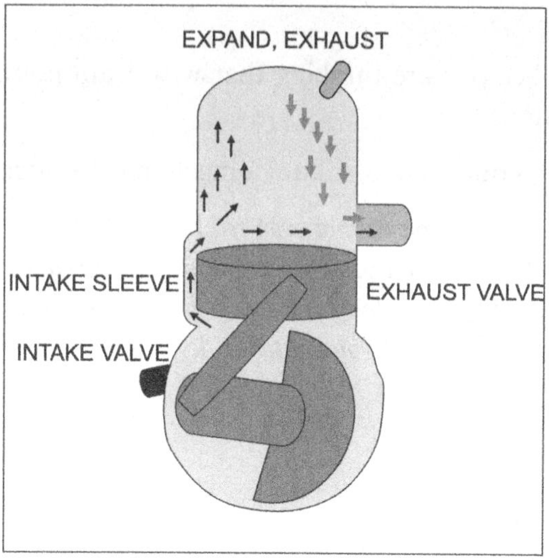

Now if we look at a four-stroke engine, there is a fundamental difference in the design. The crankcase is isolated here. Also, valves remain closed during compression and power strokes. At any one time, only one of the valves is open. Out of four, only one stroke is the power stroke, but a four-cylinder arrangement where power strokes are 90 degrees apart makes for a smoother drive.

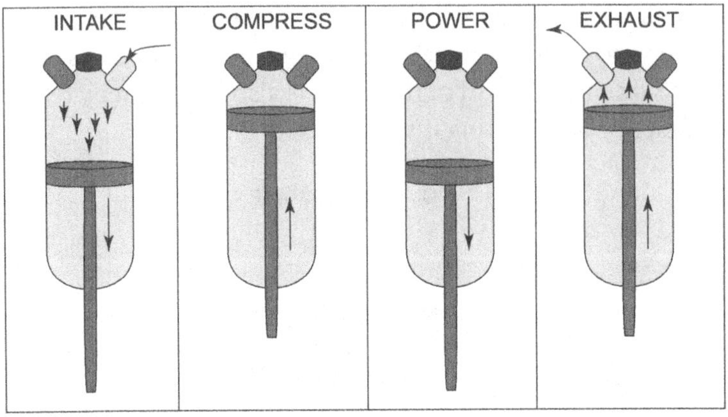

Interviewer: How does an aircraft engine look like?

Sid: Jet engines are simpler. There are no moving parts like the piston, crankshaft, etc. They work on Newton's third law of motion. Air is sucked into the engine, compressed, and then mixed with fuel to ignite it. The burnt gases escape out of a nozzle providing propulsion or thrust to the aircraft. They are pretty much like rocket engines in their working principle.

Interviewer: I bet you are thinking that why I am not asking you any computer questions.

Sid (*smiling*): Of course no, Sir, I am a mechanical student after all.

(Interviewer: Poor thing, you cannot even tell the truth! I can very well see from your dropping enthusiasm that you are not happy with the questions being asked. Dude, unhappy you might be, but I have to grill you to get a little understanding of your subject knowledge and your patience level. Let me pull your leg on this reply.)

Interviewer: In that case, shall I interpret that you are not interested in IT? And that you are attending this process simply because you are eligible?

Sid (*assertively*): Oh no Sir, it is not like that, certainly not. I should be able to learn and explain whatever is expected out of me. And I can quickly learn new things. Before coming here, I hardly knew anything about mechanical engineering, but I learnt it here. For that matter, I knew nothing about computers. Now I possess fairly good knowledge of the basics including computer hardware and C and C++ programming. I have also attended a database basics training …

Interviewer: What if we don't hire you?

Sid: Sir, I think you would make a final decision only after getting an understanding of my mechanical and computer knowledge, and I think I can do justice to your questions so that you will decide to select me.

Interviewer (*smiling deceptively*): Hmm … Is that funda or overconfidence?

Sid: Sir, it is neither. Believe me, it is not. It is true. Can I request you to please ask me more questions so that you can judge better?

Interviewer: You mean to say I could not judge you properly in the last fifteen minutes?

Sid (*pleading*): No, Sir, I did not mean that.

Interviewer: Then what did you mean?

Sid (*little upset*): Sorry, Sir, I was simply requesting you to ask me more questions, nothing more than that.

(Interviewer: Let me be mean with you and give you a problem that none of your friends from other institutes have even dared to think of a solution.)

Interviewer (*laying the trap*): All right, let me accept your request. You see this figure. It is a square inside a square inside a square and so on. Write a C program to find the total area of all the squares.

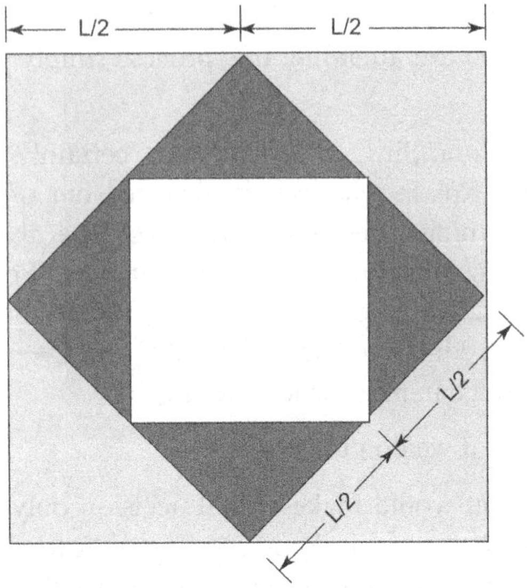

Sid: Give me few minutes please, let me think of the logic for this one.

Interviewer: Please take your time! But do tell me the logic before you start writing the code.

(Interviewer: You have not immediately refused to try it out like others had done! At least your attitude toward problem solving looks good. I will select you for sure if you can give me the correct code!)

Sid: I would want my program to solve this problem in the same manner as I would solve it on a piece of paper. So the approach here is to find the sum of a geometric progression for which the first term is L^2. I need to find out the common ratio here.

Interviewer: Why do you think it should be a geometric progression and not an arithmetic progression?

Sid: The side is decreasing successively by nth factor, not by a constant number. Hence the need to go for geometric progression. Here the second square side is $[(L/2)^2 + (L/2)^2]^{1/2} = L/\sqrt{2}$

So the second square's area is $L^2/2$.

For the third square we can see that side is $L/2$ and area is $L^2/4$.

Now, ½ is the common ratio. So sum of this series would be

Sum $= L^2 / (1 - ½) = 2L^2$.

Shall I write the program which will accept a and r and give the sum of the geometric series?

Interviewer: No, I don't think that you should simplify it to this extent. You see this slightly modified diagram here. The new square is formed by joining 0.4 times the length of the two sides. In this manner, there can be any variation. So, you should write code for that generic situation.

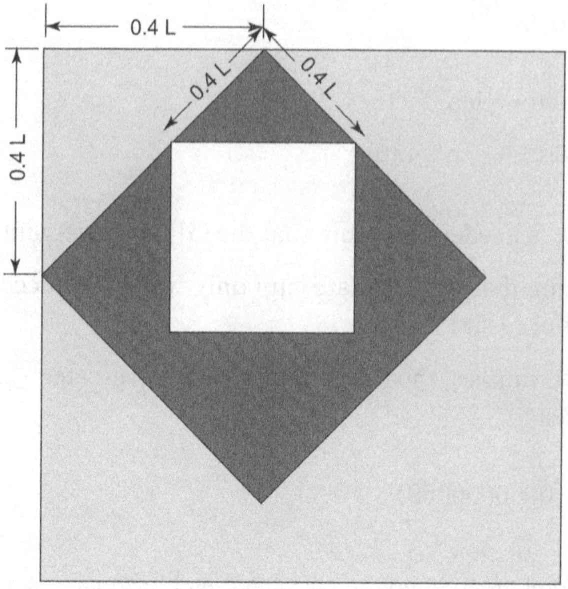

Sid: Sure Sir, let me write it out first, then I will explain the code line by line.

```
/***************************************************************/
#include <stdio.h>
#include <conio.h>

int main()
{

float len_factor, ratio, total_area;

printf("Enter the factor (in decimal format only) by which the side of the next square reduces \n");
```

```
scanf("%f", &len_factor);

/* Assume the first square side is 1 unit.

Then the next square side becomes [ len_factor X √2 ]

So the next square area becomes [ len_factor X len_factor X 2 ]

As the first square area is 1, this second square area also becomes the common ratio */

ratio = len_factor * len_factor * 2;

printf("Ratio is : %f \n", ratio);

/* This check is needed to ensure that the GP is convergent.

This will ensure that we calculate sum only when the successive squares become smaller in size.

A value of 1 implies the area remains same, greater than 1 implies increasing area */

if (ratio >= 1.0000000000)
{
        printf("Total area cannot be calculated as the squares are getting bigger
\n");
}
else
{
        total_area = 1 / (1 - ratio);   //GP sum to infinity formula
        //total_area has to be multiplied by L Square to get actual total area

 printf("                                        2\n");
 printf("Total area of all the squares is : L   * f\n", total_area);
 }

 return 0;
 }
/*************************************************************/
```

(Interviewer to himself: I definitely like the 'if' clause. Your aptitude does look good!)

Interviewer: Very good, Sid. But what is the second-last printf statement doing there?

Sid: Sir, it is a manual arrangement to make the number 2 of the L square appear as a superscript.

Interviewer: Ah ... smart boy! Next take this problem and give me a program for its solution.

Problem: I want to list all the 4-digit numbers that can be formed using four given distinct natural numbers.

Sid: I am not sure of the logic here but I think we can do it using an array. Let me try it out.

```
/****************************************************/
#include <stdio.h>
#include <conio.h>
void main()
{
    int num, i,j,k,l, arr[4];
    printf("Enter the 4 digits separated by space \n");
    scanf("%d %d %d %d" , &arr[0], &arr[1], &arr[2], &arr[3]);

    printf("Entered numbers are: %d %d %d %d \n", arr[0], arr[1], arr[2],
arr[3]);

    printf("The list of all possible numbers is : \n");

    for (i=0; i<=3 ; i++ )
    {
        for (j=0; j<=3 ; j++ )
        {
            for (k=0; k<=3 ; k++ )
            {
                for (l=0; l<=3 ; l++ )
```

```
                        {
                                if (!(k == l || j==k || j==l || i==j || i==k ||
i==l))
                                {
                                num = arr[i] * 1000 + arr[j] * 100 + arr[k] *
10 + arr[l] * 1
                                printf("Number is %d\n", num);
                        }
                }
            }
        }
}
/************************************************************/
```

Sid: The logic here is to store the numbers entered in an array format and then set up a loop to display the individual elements of the array in different orders.

The if statement suppresses the displays where any element of the array is being referred to more than once.

The limitation of this program is that it can display permutations only for 4-digit numbers. We need to include an extra loop if any higher number of digits is required. For that I think we need to write a basic permutation function, which can generate permutations of two numbers. This function can then be called again and again, not sure if that would be a recursive call though.

(Sid to himself: I am impressed with myself that I could think of the equality check and include it here. Wish I could think of that dynamic logic also that would have enabled this code to run for any digit numbers!)

Interviewer: I think this will work for now. Do you have any experience with file handling?

Sid: Yeah, I have basic knowledge of file handling.

Interviewer: Well in that case, can you write the code for this problem:

Problem: There is a file called as record.csv. Every day a line has to be added to it in the format:

"Date: Current Date, Number of students present is: Number of students present"

Number of students present is supplied as an input.

Sid: Yeah, I can do that.

```
/***************************************************/
#include <stdio.h>
#include <time.h>

void main()
{
	int students;
	char filename[15]="record.csv", datevar[10];
	_strdate(datevar);
	FILE *fp;

	printf("\n Enter the number of students present today \n");
	scanf("%d" , &students);

	fp = fopen(filename,"a");
	if(fp == NULL)
printf("File Open Error");
	fprintf(fp,"%s%s%s%d%s","\nDate : ", datevar, ", Number of students
present is: ",students, "\n");
	fclose(fp);
}
/***************************************************/
```

Interviewer: Please explain the program line by line.

Sid: Sure, Sir.

1. The stdio.h file is included for the standard I/O functions. In this program, printf, scanf, fopen, fclose, fprintf, and fscanf are such functions.
2. time.h is included for the _strdate function.
3. Coming to the code, _strdate function returns the current date in

string format. So it needs a string pointer to assign the date string value.

4. fp is the pointer to the FILE structure, which is also defined in the stdio.h file.
5. Then the number of students is received as input.
6. After this the file record.csv is opened in append mode and we check if the file could really be opened or not.
7. Next, using the fprintf statement, we write all the required data into the file that was successfully opened for append. The format string is the same as we use in normal printf function.
8. Finally, the file is closed through fclose function. Now this file can be accessed by other applications.

Interviewer: All right. What will happen if the length of datevar is reduced to 5?

Sid: I think it would throw an error as the date string is 8 characters long and one additional place is needed for the string termination null character. But there is no bound checking in C, so it might be possible that it gives no error and directly overwrites some other data in the memory. But I believe some provision should be made in strdate to check the string size and not to overwrite.

Interviewer: Hmm. You must have been very young then, but do you understand the hugely hyped Y2K problem?

Sid: Yeah, I know about it. It was the problem about handling dates when the century changed. Many times dates are written with two characters for the year part. Also, the base century being considered was 1900. So the basic problem was that the year 2000 would be interpreted as year 1900. And almost all systems work on dates. Like our credit cards, mobile balance, flight schedules, etc.

Interviewer: And how about the Y2K+10 problem, the problem associated with year 2010?

Sid: It is a problem associated with the representation of numbers in decimal or hexadecimal format. So some systems interpreted 10 as 10, while others interpreted it as 16 and that created the problem.

Interviewer: Very well done, Sid! I am pleased to let you know that you are through ☺

Sid: Thanks, Sir. I was a bit nervous for a while. Thank you.

Interviewer: You are welcome, Sid. Have a good day!

(Interviewer: Bye, bye, Mr. Yeah.)

Sid: Sir, I want to tell you something before I go out.

Interviewer: Please go ahead.

Sid: Sir, I really enjoyed this discussion. I am so happy that you gave programming scenarios we generally don't look into and I could solve them. And also, I felt very good recollecting the mechanical concepts I had seen at work during my summer training with Eicher Motors. ☺

Interviewer: I am happy to hear that. I thought you would be cursing me throughout the day for grilling you.

Sid: Not at all, Sir.

SCENE 3

As Sid shares his interesting interview experience with the others waiting and warns them that the interviewer is a solid man, not to be taken for a ride, the interviewer marks these lines:

Siddhartha's evaluation – Select.

Aptitude – Very Good.

Computer Knowledge – Pretty good for a mechanical student.

Discipline Knowledge – Very Good. Understands the basic concepts.

Communication – Good; error-free diction.

General – Very well read and aware of his surroundings.

SCENE 4

Hello dear diary, my constant travel companion, I will tell you about a kid called Sid today.

Sid is a complete dude, I have committed him to my memory as the "Yeah Man." We need smart people to handle our demanding customers and I am sure he will win over the nastiest of them. He is smart; he could greet me in a charming manner even though he had to almost barge into the room. And he did not forget to appreciate my efforts spent in collecting interesting interview questions.

He is strong in aptitude; he is the CAT-cracking material. On top of that, he is technically sound, both in his discipline and in programming. He understands concepts really well and this understanding is sure to take him a long way. His technical brilliance will be an asset to his team.

I am happy that despite all these positives, he is not short-tempered. I could see that he was upset during the stress test but not to the extent that everyone around could easily make that out.

And my personal favorite has been his confident taskmaster attitude. You know how many students had refused to even think, leave apart code, when they had seen that square-area problem diagram, but he attacked it at full throttle!

Will talk to you 'morrow,

Good Night

* * *

6

MCA's Yash is Grilled by Ocean Intelligence

SCENE 1

Bytes from the fellow students have assured Yash that the OI team is focusing on communication skills and that happens to be his strong area. He is thinking of ways to strike and sustain an interesting conversation with the interviewer. And, most importantly, he plans to wear that charming smile of his throughout the interview to convey his confidence and ease.

SCENE 2

Yash is called out by the interviewer himself and he notices his confident gait and pleasing manners immediately …

Yash (*smiling charmingly*): Good afternoon, Sir!

Interviewer: Good afternoon, Yash! What is the secret of your confidence?

Yash (*completely knocked out*): Sir … umm …

Interviewer: What, you don't want to disclose?

Yash (*reassured*): Nothing like that, Sir, it's just that even I don't know.

(Interviewer: Why do you hesitate to mention subject knowledge, experience with multitude of programming languages, awards, or any of the technical strengths your CV is bragging about as the reason? I smell a rat here!)

Interviewer: Hmm … you …

Yash (*interrupting*): Sir, I think it is because of public speaking; I have been participating in debates, anchoring programs, etc., from a very early age.

Interviewer: That's wonderful! What was the last topic you debated?

Yash (*charged with excitement*): We held a debate on the environmental impacts of GM crops in India.

Interviewer: That must have been a very interesting and heated discussion, I guess!

Yash: Yes Sir, it was.

Interviewer: Tell me as a computer technologist, why can't we do extensive data mining on the past impacts of those crops and draw a predictive model based on that?

Yash (*feeling punched in face*): …

Interviewer: You have studied about data mining, haven't you?

Yash: Yes … we have.

Interviewer: Not to worry about that. Can you write a program to demonstrate operator overloading in C++?

Yash (*thinking for few seconds and giving up*): Sorry, Sir.

Interviewer: How is function overloading handled in C?

Yash: Sir, it is not supported.

Interviewer: Then how can printf and scanf functions accept variable number of arguments?

Yash (*shaking head*): …

Interviewer: Well how is function overloading handled in C++?

Yash: That is through virtual functions. We need to precede the function name by virtual keyword.

Interviewer: What is the Java destructor syntax?

Yash (*scratching memory really hard*): Sorry, Sir, I don't remember reading about it in Java.

Interviewer: List down the sequence of activities that will happen when a child destructor is invoked in C++?

Yash (*confused*): It will execute the destructor code …

Interviewer: The question was about which, self or parent?

Yash: Self, no parent hmm no, I think self …

Interviewer (*banteringly*): Can there be any other option?

Yash: …

Interviewer: Tell me how are C pointers and structures different from C++ pointers and structures?

Yash (*acting smart*): Sir, C++ is based on OOP concepts, everything is considered an object in C++, whereas it is not so in C …

Interviewer (*derisively*): Very important difference indeed! What would be the output for this program?

```
/*************************************************************/
abstract final class Top{
int i;
abstract final void display();
}
class Display extends Top {
        Display() {
super();
}
        display() {
                System.out.println(i);
        }

public static void main (String[] args) {
        Display d = new Display();
        d.display();
}
/*************************************************************/
```

Yash (*thinking for a minute*): It will print a garbage value.

Interviewer: Hmm ...

Yash: Is that right, Sir?

Interviewer: That you should know, not me! Suppose for your project, you have to create an online application for a client. Which of the web technologies would you prefer to use and why?

Yash: Sir I think the client will tell which one he wants to use. It depends on license fees.

Interviewer: And how will the client decide which one they want to use?

Yash: Sorry, Sir ...

Interviewer: See Yash, be frank and let me know if I ask you any questions from the technologies not included in your curriculum, OK?

Yash (*half-heartedly*): OK.

Interviewer: What are the various memory management schemes used in OS?

Yash: Paged memory management, demand-paged memory management, segmented memory management, ...

Interviewer: Which of these schemes is used for managing virtual memory?

Yash: Virtual memory ... not sure, Sir.

Interviewer: What is cyclomatic complexity and what is regression testing?

Yash: Sir, we have it in this semester, it is not yet studied.

Interviewer: Can you write a shell script to read a list of file names from another file and combine their data in sorted order?

Yash: Sir, I know "cat" command is used for combining. "sort" is used for sorting data. To write a script ... these commands need to be used; I am not getting the script right now.

Interviewer: Do you have any idea how to make a shell script variable value accessible to another shell script?

Yash: Sorry, Sir, I have not written many scripts.

Interviewer: Can you tell me why do we need to install a printer driver while an external hard disk drive needs none?

Yash: May be because one hard disk is already installed …

Interviewer: Do you know that to connect to two different printers, you still need to install two drivers?

Yash: …

Interviewer: What is VPN?

Yash (*enthusiastically*): VPN stands for virtual private network. It makes a part of the public Internet appear private by encapsulating data packets sent over network through a firewall. Thus two parties can communicate securely with each other after installing the firewalls at their respective ends.

(Interviewer: Ahh … you came well prepared for this one, what if I ask you about the meaning of each of the fancy terms you have used!)

Interviewer: That sounds very technical and very good. That was my last question for you. Now you can shoot questions, if you have any!

Yash: No, Sir. Have a good day!

Interviewer: Thank you. You too have a good day!

SCENE 3

The interviewer marks Yash as rejected.

Programming Skills – Poor

Subject Knowledge – Poor

Communication – Very Good

SCENE 4

One of the interviewer's nieces has recently joined MCA and she asks him for tips to prepare for interview as he visits her on the weekend. The interviewer is delighted to guide her at such an early phase as she will get enough time to prepare well. He tells her:

"I recently rejected a nicely talking MCA student because he was more of an empty suit. He had a very superficial technical knowledge, the sort of knowledge gained by reading thin refresher books just before the exams. I questioned him on a broad range of topics from his syllabus and he displayed poor application knowledge throughout. For example, you know what are drivers but don't know why and when are they used, you know what is memory management, but not quite sure which type of memory is being managed.

Lack of programming practice was another reason he was confused when asked about programs. Imagine, he got confused when asked for the destructor syntax in Java which is nonexistent and not required or could not identify a simple mistake of declaring a class as both abstract and final!

The thing is, the way people on this earth look different from each other, they think different from each other. To imagine what question an interviewer can ask a student at any time of the year is like trying to beat the best random question generator machine on the planet. So, for getting through a technical interview, there is only one shortcut. Study at leisure, understand concepts, and look out for correlation with real world objects and practice programs."

❋ ❋ ❋

7

Computer's Raman's Ordeal at MicroMatics

SCENE 1

Today Raman is appearing for his 10th interview. Fear of rejection reaching double digits is written large on his face. His silent prayers are requesting for an easy interviewer. He knows the painful truth that MicroMatics is a company that pays a lot of emphasis to communication skills, yet he is hoping for a miraculous exception to happen. He is trying hard to recollect whatever he has studied till now. He is trying harder to remember the valuable tips offered by campus gurus on favorite subjects and handling the interview. As he glances again at the paper on which someone has written a flattering introduction for him, his turn to face the ordeal finally arrives.

SCENE 2

Raman (*uneasy*): Good morni … sorry, good afternoon, M'am.

Interviewer: Good afternoon. You are Raman Dhiren from computers, isn't it?

(Raman nods in agreement.)

Interviewer (*smiling*): Take a seat, please.

Raman (*nervous*): Thank you, M'am.

Interviewer: How are you?

Raman (*almost trembling*): Good, M'am.

Interviewer: Can you tell me something?

Raman: Yes, M'am.

Interviewer (*very grave*): Have you stolen someone's money and police is coming behind you?

Raman (*bewildered and vigorously shaking head in denial*): No … M'am, no! Interviewer: You are sure of that, right?

Raman (*confused*): Yes, M'am!

Interviewer (*smiling*): Then why are you so nervous? You have done no wrong as you said. So you shouldn't be scared of me or anyone else. Is this your first interview?

Raman: No, M'am.

Interviewer: Then relax, you already know that interviewers don't hit or rag. Anyways, how is the fresher ragging scene in this institute? Were you ragged a lot as a fresher?

Raman (*suddenly confident*): No ragging these days, M'am, no ragging at all! Even during our time, there was not much ragging, there were some introduction sessions only. How will the seniors help if they don't know the freshers. So for that only some sessions are there.

(Interviewer: You said that much for justifying ragging! Anyways good to learn that you can reply in more than two words, in fact, say complete sentences also.)

Interviewer: I see that you enjoyed giving introductions. Would you introduce yourself once again now if you won't call it ragging?

Raman: Yes, M'am, definitely…

Interviewer (*pretending anger*): What, you will definitely call it ragging?

Raman (*smiling*): No, M'am. I will definitely give my introduction. This is Raman Dhiren, final-year Computer Science student at the RPSIT. About my family, my father is in government job, UP government, my mother is a housewife, and my younger brother is in twelfth standard. I completed my plus 2 from UP board from Phulpur near Allahabad and got 84 percent marks. My interests are gardening and listening to music.

Interviewer: Next time say your mother is a homemaker, OK?

Raman: Yes, M'am.

(Raman (*regretting*): Oh God, I forgot most of that intro which was written for this company by the campus guru and said the regular stuff! How could I remember just the last two lines?)

Interviewer: Very good. Is this place near to Mirzapur also?

Raman: Yes, M'am.

Interviewer: If I am not mistaken, it is a very significant place. Can you tell me what the significance of the place is?

Raman: M'am, it is a central place for India, and IST, the Indian Standard Time, is calculated from here.

Interviewer: I remember that now. Why don't the bonsai grow in height?

Raman: Hmm ... sorry, M'am.

Interviewer: What do you do in gardening?

Raman: I have got some fern plants and some medicinal plants from the nursery.

(Raman: At least I could remember that much!)

Interviewer: Why are ferns so commonly used as ornamental plants?

Raman: Sorry, M'am.

Interviewer: How are ferns different from regular plants? And also, tell me the scientific names of the medicinal plants you tend to in your garden.

Raman: Sorry, M'am. And for names, I only know English names ... aloe vera, basil, ...

Interviewer: Now tell me the truth; are you really interested in gardening?

Raman (*trembling again*): M'am, actually I was preparing for the interview and a friend gave suggestion. I am sorry, M'am.

Interviewer: That means you have no thought process of your own and you completely follow your friends even if they are wrong?

(Interviewer: Raman, I want to reject you, but somehow I am not able to justify that till now, for how much more time will I have to listen to your friends' tape recorder? Done, one more cooked-up story and you will be out!)

Raman (*shaking again*): No, M'am. I am sorry.

Interviewer: You don't need to say sorry to me. Just try to give honest replies from now onward.

Raman (*shaking again*): Yes, Ma'm.

Interviewer: By the way, you must have been a brilliant student to score 84 percent in UP board! You didn't mention your college percentage though! What is your percentage till seventh semester?

Raman: 6.7 CGPA.

Interviewer: Why has that happened? You don't like college subjects?

Raman: No M'am, not like that. Actually I had problem in adjusting to English here. I studied Hindi Medium till plus 2, that's why. Till third semester, I got very less marks, after that I improved on that.

Interviewer: You have studied in Hindi medium till 12th?

Raman: Yes, M'am.

Interviewer: Then I must say you have worked really hard on improving your English.

Raman: Yes, M'am. In second sem, I joined a coaching institute also. Now I read English books and talk in English for more improvement.

(Interviewer: He has been nervous on and off but communication is OK, at least I could follow what he said without extra efforts, let me invest some time now to gauge his technical capability.)

Interviewer: Very good! Let's talk about some technical stuff now. See these two code pieces and tell me the output they will generate.

Code A:

```
void main()
{
    int i=1, j=0;
    if (i)
        printf("Inside I");
    if (j)
        printf("Inside J");
}
```

CODE B:

```
class IFTest {public static void main()
{
        int i=0, j=1;
        if (i)
                System.out.println("Inside I");
        if (j)
                System.out.println("Inside J");
}}
```

Raman: Code A will always print "Inside I" and code B will print "Inside J."

Interviewer: And if I say that these programs won't even compile, then?

Raman: Let me see again please.

Code A is C code … simple statements and there is no semicolon after the if condition. For Code A, I don't think there will be any compilation error.

Code B is Java, the System class is also written properly. This will also compile fine, M'am.

Interviewer: That's fine. Please tell me the reasons for differences between these two programs.

Raman: M'am, the first program is a C program. C is a procedural language and there is no class concept in C. Java is object oriented. So we need to encapsulate Java programs in classes.

We need to define the main method as public so that external JVM can call it.

Next is the difference in print statements. C uses printf function. Java has println method defined in the System Class.

M'am, yes, the Java code is not going to compile …

Interviewer: Why all of a sudden?

Raman: M'am, the Java if condition needs a Boolean value, but here an integer value is used, which will throw error. Actually M'am, we have to study so many languages and then everything gets mixed …

Interviewer: I see ... what is the role of keyword static?

Raman: Static means no need for class object. That means main can be called directly without creating an instance of the class object in which it is defined. So I see it like this: declaring main as public static brings it out of the compulsory class in which it is declared.

Interviewer: Can you use public static modifiers for the C main() also?

Raman: Public, no. It has no meaning in C. Static is for C variables, not functions. No, we cannot use static with main.

Interviewer: What is a static variable in C?

Raman: Static variable value remains constant; it is not destroyed even when the control goes out of the block it is defined in.

Interviewer: So in this code, either we will see the line "I is 1" two times or we will get a compilation error as 'i' is being incremented, isn't it?

```
void main() {
print_fun();
print_fun(); }

void print_fun(){
static int i=1;
printf("I is %d", i++);}
```

Raman: It should print "I is 1" and then "I is 2". 'i' is not destroyed when the control goes out of the function print_fun.

Interviewer: But you said value remains constant!

Raman: Yes M'am, I meant, value remains there even when control is lost, I should say value persists.

Interviewer (*flipping through CV*): Raman, your project description has made me very curious. You seem to have done some good work to fine traffic violators in a transparent manner. Tell me honestly, did the system impose a fine on you also?

Raman (*smiling*): Not yet M'am, it is still not fully functional.

Interviewer: Please explain me this complete system.

Raman: M'am, our project has two modules, the electronics module and the software module. I am in software module. Two friends from electronics are working on the electronics module. I will first explain the electronic module ...

Interviewer: Before that you explain what this system is about? What is the purpose of this system?

Raman: M'am, we are building an automated challan system. When traffic police will catch someone, for example, crossing speed limit, a challan form will automatically open on their system. Now the police inspector has to enter his details like his badge number and name and also the driver's name, license number, and which rule was broken. Then he has to submit the form. He will get a registration number, which he will give to the driver. Then he will keep the license with him and let the driver go. Next day, the driver has to go to the court, give registration number, pay the fine, and take the license back.

So no driver can ever tell the traffic police that he has no money. Also the traffic police cannot strike a deal because once the form is opened, it has to be submitted, or else the traffic police will also have to pay fine. And the best part is that the driver has to go to the court to take his license back. People can pay fine, but the fear of going to court every time will stop lot of traffic violations.

Interviewer: Wow! That sounds amazing in theory. I cannot wait to hear how you all have implemented it!

Raman: The electronics module works on a camera. So this system has to be installed at important junctions. The camera monitors the traffic movement. So if a vehicle is flagged by the inspector, the inspector will drive after it, and the vehicle will slow down and then come toward the camera. The video is analyzed and if it decides that it was a traffic violation case, the challan form is opened on the system. I don't have much idea about this module working. I can only draw the block diagram of this module.

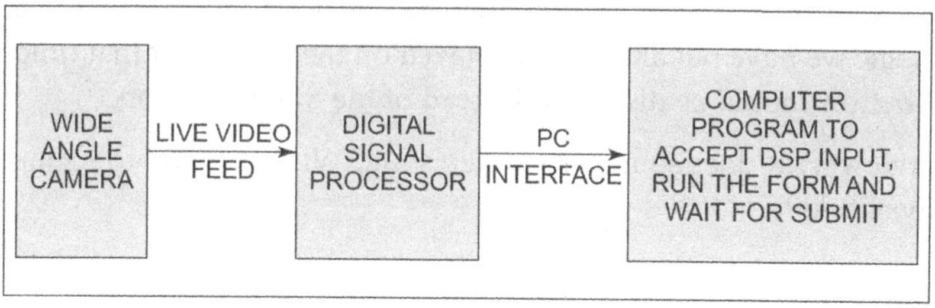

In the computer module, we have to create the back-end database, design the form GUI, and put logic in the button to check and store the values in the database. The form GUI is simple with these fields:

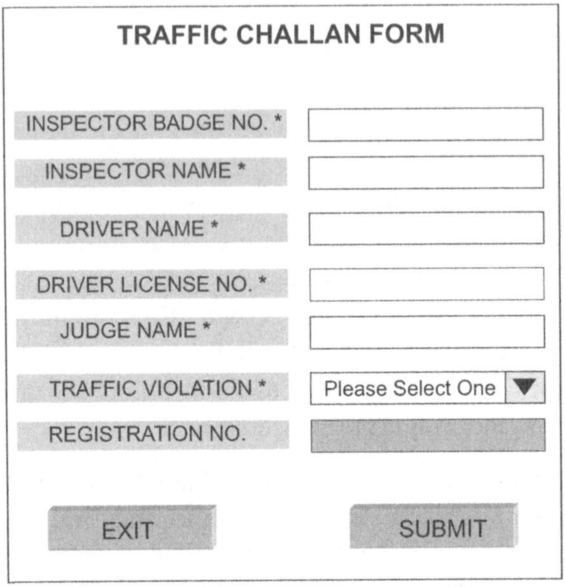

But the main challenge we faced was in validation. As soon as the badge number is filled and the field loses focus, we need to check if the entered value is present in the INSPECTOR table in the central database or not. Accordingly, we need to change the color of the box to green if it was found or pop up an error message and change the text box color to red.

If badge number was correct, the inspector name should be filled from back-end only.

The same has to be checked for judge name also. We have a JUDGE table also. On top of that, it is possible that the value matches, but not the case, so we need to automatically correct that also.

Then we need to check if all the fields are filled when submitting the form. After that, the registration number is generated based on the back-end logic we have put and then displayed on the screen. At that time, the Exit button should be displayed instead of the Submit button.

Interviewer: It does sound very interesting. Who told you to include so many checks?

Raman: Our guide sir gave us list of requirements. Checks are also in that list. He also asked us to do this in Java.

Interviewer: How do you read values from the database? If I understood you right, you plan to keep the database remote at a central place so that everyone can access it.

Raman: Guide sir has done jdbc setup for us, though we don't know about it till now.

Interviewer: That's fine, but you are doing this project inside your computer lab where all systems are on network. But how will you provide high-speed network access at a traffic junction?

Raman: That is the problem, M'am. Guide sir told us not to think much about that as our basic purpose for doing this project is to learn how to do a real-time application development. He said we should just consider that as a scenario right now. When the system starts working in our college lab, then he will think what to do after that.

Interviewer: How many people are working on the computers module?

Raman: M'am, two.

Interviewer: OK, So tell me what has been your contribution to this module?

Raman: M'am, I did not work on the database setup. I only worked on the GUI design and validation part. I tried and tested lot of code for that and finally could manage a functional front-end. Also got help from guide sir for the first validation. Reading the value by executing SQL on the database from the Java class file was bit difficult for me, so sir helped me on that one.

Interviewer: You would do yourself a big help if you can write a part of that code right now. Here's the paper!

Raman: Yes, M'am, I can write that. Before that, I want to draw a flowchart to explain the logic.

Interviewer: That would be even better. Please go ahead.

Raman: I will at first take the Inspector Badge Number input box only. The main activities for it to work are:

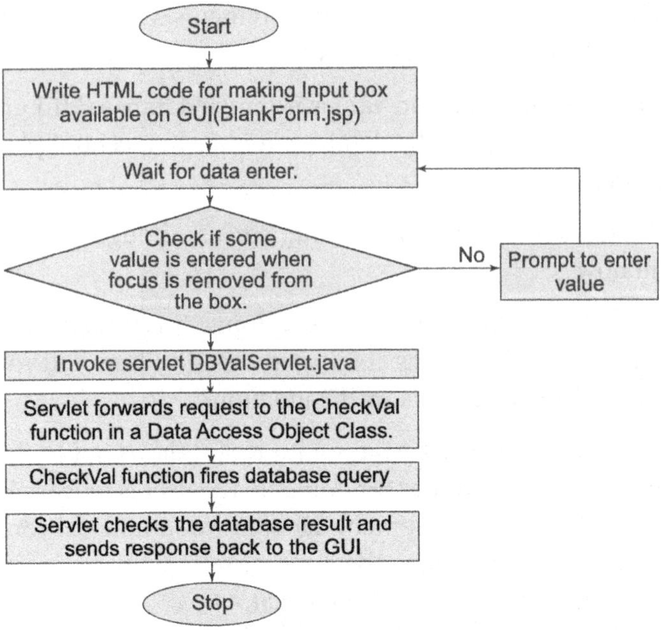

The code for BlankForm.jsp is somewhat like this:

```
/*****************************************************************/
<HTML>
<HEAD>
<%@ page
import="java.io.*, java.util.*, java.sql.*, com. view.MessageVB"
errorPage="error.jsp"
language="java"
contentType="text/html; charset=ISO-8859-1"%>

<script type="text/javascript">
        function SubmitValue (TableName, FieldName, VarName) {
                TableName = TableName;
                FieldName = FieldName;
                FieldVal = document.getElementById(VarName);
                if{FieldVal.value == " ")
                        alert{'Please enter value in the field' + VarName);
                else
                        document.thisForm.submit(); }
```

```
18  </script>
19
20  <H1> TRAFFIC CHALLAN FORM</H1>
21  </HEAD>
22
23  <BODY>
24  <p><font class="pageTitle"><b>TRAFFIC CHALLAN FORM<b></font></p>
25  <FORM name="BlankForm" action="DBValServlet" method="post">
26  <TABLE>
27      <TR>
28              <TD><input type="text" value="INSPECTOR BADGE NO. *"
                id='IBN'></TD>
29              <TD><input type="text" value="id= 'BadgeNo' onBlur=
                "SubmitValue ('INSPECTOR', 'BADGE', 'BadgeNo')"></TD>
30      </TR>
31  </TABLE>
32  </FORM>
33  </BODY>
34  </HTML>
```

/***/

1. We can start from line 25. This form is called BlankForm and invokes the DBValServlet class on post.
2. Table Data on line 29 describes the input box for accepting the Badge No. It is given id "BadgeNo." This input box calls the function SubmitValue when it loses focus. We have onBlur event to detect that.
3. SubmitValue is a reusable function, which is taking three values. Table Name and Attribute Name are the first two parameters. They are used to generate query for the database in a DAO class afterward. The id is the third parameter for this function. Right now we can see these three values ("INSPECTOR," "BADGE," "BadgeNo"). If it is called from Judge Name, then we can just change these values.
4. Now we go to this function on line 10. JavaScript is used to write the function code. Another point here is we are writing this function in the header part of the form because it will be called on many events, not just form load.
5. Here we access the input value through "getElementById" method and then check if it is blank. It pops a message if it is

blank. Otherwise, the servlet described in form action is invoked. Now starts the database work.

6. The servlet code is written as follows:

```
/**********************************************************/
package com.servlet;
import: javax.servlet.*;
import javax.servlet.http.*;
import java.io.*;
import java.date.CheckValueDAO.Java;
public class EBValServlet extends GenericServlet {
    protected CheckValueBean processRequest(
        RHttpServletRequest req,
        HttpServletResponse resp)
        throws ServletException, IOException {
        CheckValueBean vbean = new ChkValBean();
        String TableName = req.getParameter("TableName");
        String FieldName = req.getParameter("FieldName");
        String FieldVal = req.getParameter("FieldVal") ;
        CheckValueDAO ChkVaLDAO = new CheckValueDAO();
        vbean = ChkValDAO.CheckVal(TableName, FieldName, FieldVal);
        switch (vbean.getResultState()) {
            case ChkValBean.SUCCESS :
                vbean.setNextURL("SubmitForm.jsp");
                break;
            case ChkValBean.FAILURE :
                vbean.setNextURL("BlankForm. jsp");
                break;
        }
```

```

            return vbean;
        }
    }

```

/**/

7. DBAValServlet class has the method processRequest and it returns another class CheckValueBean. Sir asked us to handle all value passing through a single bean class. I am yet to understand it properly.
8. getParameter method reads the values sent from the form.
9. Then it invokes the CheckVal method. This method is in the ChkValDAO class. All database queries are written in this class.
10. If the database query fails, we come back to the page BlankForm. If it is successful, then another form is displayed, which is nothing but the SubmitForm.
11. Actually next form is displayed only when all the database queries are successful; there is another if-else logic that maintains control on the BlankForm only if the form is not fully filled.

Raman: Shall I write the database class code also?

Interviewer: Yes, if you can.

Raman: Yes, M'am.

/**/

```
public class ApproveReport-DAO {

public int CheckVal(String TableName, String FieldName, String FieldVal)
throws DataException
{
        ConnectionOpen conn = getDBConnection();
        try {

                Statement stmt = com.createStatement() ;

                String sqlstmt = "select * from" + TableName +
                        "where" + FieldName + "= " + FieldVal;
```

```
12
13              String rset = executeQuery(sqlstmt, stint);
14
15              if ('1' .equals (rset))
16                      ChkValBean.setResultState = "SUCCESS";
17              else
18                      ChkValBean.setResultState = "FAILURE";
19
20          catch (SQLException ex) {
21                  throw new DataException(ex);
22
23          } finally {
24                  conn.close();
25          }
26
27   }
28   }
29
/*************************************************************/
```

M'am, in this class method, we open the database connection. The query is dynamically formed for all tables on line 10.

Then it is executed and the result is stored in the ResultSet object rset.

M'am, the return type for CheckVal function should be an array, not int.

It should be public ~~int~~ ChkValResult[] CheckVal(). We have created that array also in another class.

This is how this project is working for us.

Interviewer: Please explain the terms "throws," "try," "catch," and "finally."

Raman: M'am, these terms provide a way to handle exceptions in Java. If we see the DAO class, when connecting to database or running query, we might get database errors. So to handle those errors, the DB statements are written inside the try block. This means we expect some problems here and are ready to handle them ourselves and code execution should continue after that.

So after the try block, we have written the catch block for JVM to do handle exceptions how we want. M'am, there should be a closing curly bracket for the try block, I missed that.

After this, we are telling the JVM to convert the SQL exception to data exception and throw it to calling program. "throws" tells the calling program that this class might throw exception.

After this, the database connection should be closed. So that is written in the "finally" block. Whether an exception is raised or not in the try block, when it ends, finally block code is run.

Interviewer: Raman, your group is really doing their project! I know the lines you have written won't work if I simply copy them because of small misses here and there, but that is the unimportant 20 percent I would say. That means you could get it right 80 percent and that is amazing!

Raman: Thank you, M'am. We have spent lot of time on this.

Interviewer: Do you know UNIX commands?

Raman: Yes, M'am. Many of them I know.

Interviewer: See, I have these 10 files in a directory. I want to only see the files that begin with word 'file' and end with a number.

```
file101
file_new_10_60
File201
FILE301
file501.txt
new_file11
file_TEST_401
file6.txt
file5.txt
file1.txt
```

Raman: We can use 'ls' command.

ls –l file*[0-9]

* means it can be any character after file. [] is for one character. That one-character range is between 0 and 9.

Interviewer: Which files will be listed?

Raman: file101, file_new_10_60, file_TEST_401.

Interviewer: And if I want to see all files which start with word 'File' and case does not matter?

Raman: We can check like this:

ls -l [F,f][I,i][L,l][E,e]*

Interviewer: In files that start with word 'File' and case does not matter, some lines contain a word "Eureka." You have to count such lines in these files.

Raman: We can use 'grep' command to find matching lines.

grep -i -c "Eureka" [F,f][I,i][L,l][E,e]*

Interviewer: What are these "i" and "c" options?

Raman: "i" is used for ignore letter case. "c" is for counting.

Interviewer: And if you have to replace all occurrences of "Eureka" with "veni vidi vici" in these files?

Raman: With "sed" command, we can replace one string by another for all files at one time, otherwise will need to replace in files one by one. "g" will replace all occurrences.

sed "s/ Eureka/ veni vidi vici/g" [F,f][I,i][L,l][E,e]*

Interviewer: Very good, Raman! That's all I had to ask you. Keep on working like you did for your project. Bye.

Raman: Bye, M'am.

SCENE 3

As the interviewer completes the evaluation form, she is reminded of Raman's form layout and starts wondering about the logic being used in the feedback form. Lost in those thoughts she barely manages to complete the form when the next candidate walks in.

Raman is recommended as a Select and can be offered a position at MicroMatics.

Subjects' Knowledge:

C – Good

Java – Very Good

UNIX, DB – Good

Project Description – Very Good

Communication – Acceptable

Though not fluent in English, yet can be understood easily as he frames simple and short sentences.

Attitude – Fighter spirit, good learner and team spirited – gives due credit to others when they deserve it.

SCENE 4

After the results are announced, a visibly happy Raman meets up with the interviewer.

Raman: Hello, M'am, thank you.

Interviewer: You are welcome. And congratulations!

Raman: Thanks, M'am. Can you please give me my interview feedback, what all I need to improve etc.

Interviewer (*smiling*): You want to prepare for the next interview? You don't want to join MicroMatics?

Raman (*pleading*): No, M'am, I will definitely join. Please, M'am, please give me feedback.

Interviewer: We generally don't provide direct feedback to students. But let me do that for you. Are you ready to hear not very flattering things about yourself?

Raman: Yes, M'am, I am ready.

Interviewer: All right, let me start with the positives. You have a done a very good job in your project, I have not seen students working on such practical aspects of application development, or at least they have not been able to explain it as well as you.

You are aware of the modules you are not a part of. Unlike many others, you did not say, "I have not worked on it, so I have no idea what happens there" and that is good. That makes me believe that you can look at the complete picture and are not focused just on parts.

You understand UNIX commands, not just by their names, but by functionality and right options; you also know a lot of Java. Good subject knowledge is again a positive point. This also tells me that you would be equally good in other subjects.

And by the manner in which you were approaching the code snippets provided to you shows that you understand concepts, not just read things as they are written in books.

You have put in a lot of efforts toward improving your communication skills given your medium of instruction in school. You use small, simple sentences, which convey your thoughts clearly. I did not have to struggle to understand what you were saying.

And that also gives the impression that you are open to learning and possess a fighter spirit and that is very important.

Another thing that I noticed is that your words conveyed team spirit. You gave due credit to your guide when you could have managed without mentioning him at all.

These were the reasons why I marked you a Select!

And now about the negative points. First, it is very visible that you get nervous very soon. I had to put in lot of efforts to make you feel relaxed. Have some confidence and faith in yourself and your strengths.

I don't like fake candidates, candidates who try to show off what they don't have. For example, gardening is a very good hobby if and only if it is truly your hobby. You should be able to justify yourself. We are not looking for the super-achiever candidates all the times. We need all type of people to form balanced teams.

Another point is that you talk very less sometimes and talk normally at other times. If we had started discussing your project directly, then I think I would have got a much better impression of yours. See, initially, you were saying a mere "Yes, M'am," "No, M'am." I am not saying go over the top bragging about yourself which anyways will put off any interviewer, but at least discuss your key skills and strengths. I think you were so nervous that you forgot to say anything about that in your introduction. You explained your project in a very good manner from communication perspective also. I did not have to ask you questions to understand what you were saying, so try to talk like that at other times, too.

Don't be too upset about the negative points. I simply and honestly mentioned all the reasons that had irritated me during the initial ten minutes when I had almost decided to mark you as a reject.

You know, that's why I gave you really simple programs initially. And I was almost sure that the very interesting looking project in your CV was copied from somewhere and you knew nothing that was mentioned there. So I asked you about it with the intention of putting the last nail in the coffin.

But lo, just at the very last instant, you proved me wrong and turned the outcome of the interview 180 degrees in your favor!

I have spoken a lot already; I will let you go now.

Raman: I will definitely work on the negative points. Thanks a lot, M'am.

⁂ ⁂ ⁂

8

Mechie Techie Vivaan and Newton Networks

SCENE 1

Exuberant Vivaan's energy is contagious. His confidence is making others waiting for their turn wonder about his secret diet. In the campus, he is better known as the "jack of all trades and master of many." Everyone knows that he will crack the very first interview he appears for. Vivaan himself is fully aware of this fact but that has not made him arrogant. It looks as if he is not waiting to appear for an interview but hanging out with friends.

SCENE 2

Vivaan (*cheerful*): Very good morning, Sir! I am Vivaan from the Mechanical department. How are you doing?

Interviewer: Good morning, Vivaan. I am doing great, thanks. Why do bikes have hand clutches unlike foot clutches in car?

Vivaan (*surprised*): Sir, to help driving. The driver can safely put his legs on ground whenever needed.

Interviewer: Hmm ...Why do you want to join IT?

Vivaan: Sir, mechanical is a very interesting field, but computers excite me more. I feel very comfortable with algorithms and want to pursue an MS in Computer Science. This is why I want to join IT.

Interviewer: I see that Wikipedia and HowStuffWorks are your favorite sites. Tell me about five interesting things people are not aware of generally that you learnt there.

Vivaan: Sir, you want me to just list down the stuff I learnt or I should explain the working also?

Interviewer: I am, of course, looking for a very detailed explanation.

Vivaan (*spirited*): OK, Sir.

First, after the Fukushima earthquake, there were a lot of media reports about possible reactor meltdown and spent fuel pools' overheating. I was very curious how that was possible since the reactor must have been turned off by the moderator rods. And to be frank, the news of spent fuel rods being stored in pools sounded very funny to me. I asked many people, checked papers for explanation, but found none. Then I learnt from Wiki that even after a reactor is completely shut down, that is, after the main fuel stops splitting, the fuel rod is full of radioactive by-products of fission like cesium, strontium, iodine, etc., which have a short half-life and continue to decay. As this is a radioactive decay, it continues uncontrolled and generates the heat, which might reach up to 5 percent of the heat generated by a critical reactor. This is the reason even spent fuel rods continue to emit heat. This heat, if not removed, results in meltdown. In school, we don't get to study a chain reaction like this. There, it is simple: uranium breaks into two smaller elements, barium and krypton, and that is it.

Second learning is about the electric train system. We see an electric train collecting power from OHT lines using pantograph. I used to think why it did not arc and produce scratching sound; after all, it rubs against high-voltage lines. I got to know that the pantograph contact shoe that presses against the OHT lines is made of carbon, not metal. And another point is that the lines are zigzagged to ensure that the carbon gets scratched evenly. So the lines from pole to pole are aligned somewhat like this. There were more articles on railways that made me very interested in railways, and I decided to do my summer training in a rail coach factory.

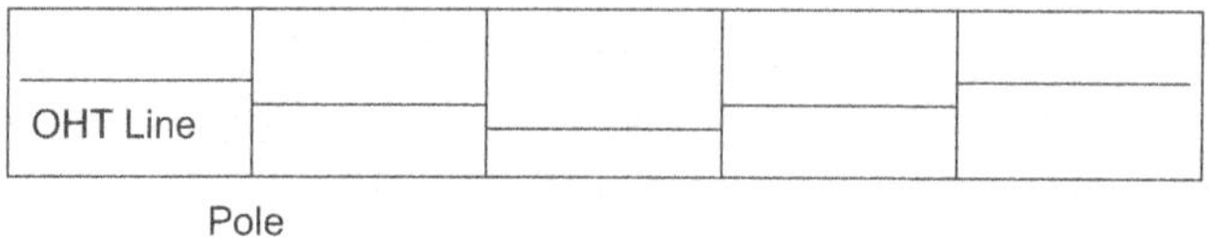

Third, I learnt about a microwave oven's working principle and its accidental discovery. It employs a device that generates high-frequency radiation that comes under microwave category, that is, the wavelength is in micrometer range. So the frequency of operation becomes a few gigahertz. These waves are easily absorbed by water and fat molecules, which start vibrating very fast. This vibration generates heat, which cooks the food. So the best part is that the food gets heated evenly. Glass and ceramics don't absorb these waves. So that gives us the microwave oven that can be conveniently used for cooking and heating. And I can proudly say I got to know this much before my electronics friends studied about this.

Next is about detecting keystrokes. How does the computer identify which key has been pressed? As opposed to the general notion, it is not the computer but the keyboard circuit that detects which key has been pressed. In that sense, a keyboard is a minicomputer by itself. There is a matrix of horizontal and vertical lines laid below the keypad but the junctions are electrically isolated. When a key is pressed, the circuit completes at that junction. And that is detected by the onboard microcontroller using a hardwired decoder circuit. This is true for laptop keyboards also. Thus the keystroke is detected and then the corresponding signal is sent to the computer. Computer checks the input key based on priority logic, where system commands like "print screen" have the highest priority. If not, the application checks if it is an application command, like "Ctrl + S." If not, it is considered as an input to the application and then we see the content being typed on screen.

And I got a lot of information about cloud computing, which is an interesting aspect of outsourcing. For example, in the traditional model of software applications, if we need some software like AutoCAD, we need to purchase and install it our machines. Our machines should also fulfill the minimum hardware requirements for installing it, like RAM, processor speed, etc. Now what happens if we switch over to the cloud model? A third-party company installs AutoCAD on its central servers and provides us with an interface to access AutoCAD on its central server. Thus, in real time, the design happens on the central server and gets stored there. So, we can use a basic computer that only needs to support the cloud interface. There are some concerns about network bandwidth, data security, etc., that are being worked out right now.

A more commonly seen example is Google Docs. The application is hosted on Google server and we get access to it through a web browser-based interface. Nothing is installed or stored on our local machines. Blogs, web-based email services, Google Translator, etc., are all services based on the cloud model.

Another interesting thing that I learnt about is fuzzy logic. I found it to be a very powerful concept. Based on a given set of inputs, it controls systems in the same manner how a person would do. We can take example of a thermostat system, which takes the set temperature as an input. Let this value be 25. First, the logic for a normal control system:

If the room temperature is higher than 25, the cooler would be switched on. It will remain on till the temperature reaches 25. Then it will switch off. Suppose the temperature continues to fall and goes below 25, the heater is switched on. This takes the temperature above 25. Now the heater is switched off and the cooler is turned on, and the cycle repeats. Equilibrium is reached through a few such oscillations in a normal control system.

Now for the fuzzy logic implementation, it does not only check the temperature difference but also the rate of change of temperature and adjusts cooling capacity or heating capacity accordingly. So a temperature of 27 will be considered hot, but just a little bit. So it would be slowly brought down to 25 and when the cooler is switched off, the temperature would have become almost constant so that the heater won't be switched on in most cases. A matrix-based approach is used to model this system and the final implementation is through digital circuit components only that work on binary logic.

We went on to implement this logic in our robotic vehicle movement control mechanism and we could bag second prize at the IIT Robotics competition.

And one more …

Interviewer: Hey Vivaan, that is very interesting to know but you know you have already given me good gyaan on six technologies by now!

Vivaan: Oh sorry, Sir, I just got carried away.

Interviewer (*smiling*): No worries, in fact you have given me my next question. I would like to know about this robot and the competition. Would you please explain that?

Vivaan: Sure, Sir. We used the chassis of a sturdy toy truck as the starting point for our robot and retrofitted it with three motors. The rear axle motor was for the purpose of driving the vehicle. The two front wheel motors are stepper motors and were used for turning purpose. On it we fitted a microcontroller board and a PCB. The PCB was fitted with three LEDs taken from the TV remote: the first for front, second for left, and third for right side. A corresponding set of IR sensors was also installed. These components were fitted at the front side of the chassis for easy detection and to avoid bumping. Then, six batteries were mounted on the rear side in two packs. The PCB had a power switch also. To move the vehicle, we place it on ground, facing the direction to move, and press the power switch. Now the vehicle starts moving around by itself by detecting obstacles and turning around.

The most important part was programming the microcontroller for detecting the obstacles and turning. I will write down the controller algorithm we used.

```
/***************************************************/
  1.  Scan the Front, Left, and Right IR sensors.
  2.  If Front Sensor is 0, then.
      2.1  If Left Motor Signal is 1, set it to 0.
      2.2  If Right Motor Signal is 1, set it to 0.
      2.3  If Rear Motor Signal is 1, Jump to Step 1.
      2.4  Else If Rear Motor Signal is 0, Set Rear Motor Signal to 1,
           Jump to Step 1.
  3.  If Left Sensor is 0, then
      3.1  If Right Motor Signal is 1, set it to 0.
      3.2  Set Left Motor signal to 1 and Jump to Step 1.
  4.  If Right Sensor is 0, then
      4.1  If Left Motor Signal is 1, set it to 0.
      4.2  Set Right Motor signal to 1 and Jump to Step 1.
  5.  Else Set Rear Motor Signal to 0. (for turning back)
  6.  If Right Motor Signal is 1, set it to 0.
  7.  Loop till Front Sensor is 1: Then Jump to 1
           Set Left Motor signal to 1
           Scan for front signal
  8.  If Right Motor Signal is 1, set it to 0.
  9.  Loop till Front Sensor is 1: Then Jump to 1
           Set Right Motor signal to 1
```

Scan for front signal

/**/

I will draw a route and explain this logic.

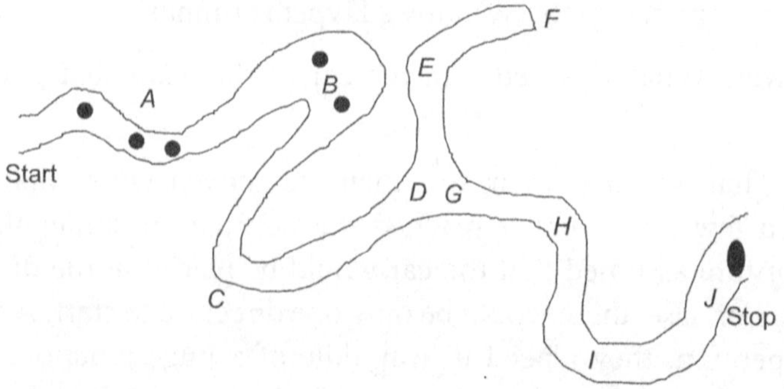

The car starts at the "Start" point and encounters an obstacle at the first circle on stretch A. Here it turns 30 degrees to right (Step 4 repeated twice through jump back to Step 1) and moves till the second circle. Here it turns left by 15 degrees (Step 3) and moves to the third circle. Here again it turns 45 degrees left and moves up to the first circle on stretch B by following steps 1 and 2. Here it slowly turns 90 degrees while still moving and reaches the second circle in an almost semicircular path.

Likewise it reaches point D which is a decision point. As we have programmed the car to turn left if the front is found closed, it simply goes over to E and F. At this point, it does not even know that there is a route on right side also. We assumed that at any such intersections on road, there will be only two ways to go, one right and one wrong. So even if the car takes a wrong turn, it will come back in a while and automatically continue moving in the right direction. Even if we take a normal road situation, there has to be an input about the route at such intersections, else even a human cannot decide which way to go.

At F it finds a dead end, turns back, and reaches G. From G, it continues moving over to H as EGH is almost a straight line.

By using concept similar to fuzzy logic in the turning steps, we weren't required to check for the actual degree of turn. Once it found an obstacle, it turned by 15 degrees in the left or right direction. If that steered it clear of the obstacle, then fine, else it turned by these many degrees again. So any turn from 15 degrees to 180 and even 360 degrees could be negotiated easily.

Interviewer: That was neat. How did you program the microcontroller?

Vivaan: Sir, I was involved in developing this algorithm and testing it for all types of routes on paper. My electronics friend translated the algorithm into code and transferred it to the controller board through a PC serial port. For that he set up the Windows HyperTerminal.

Interviewer: What was better in the car of the team that got the first prize?

Vivaan: That was the catch, Sir; their car moved worse than ours, it bumped a few times, but it reached the destination earlier than ours. Our algorithm assumed that the car would be placed in the direction of movement or, else, there would be only one direction to start. And during the competition, they placed it in middle of a huge junction. So what happened is that our car started moving in the forward direction without knowing that it could even move in other directions. And that direction had nasty turns and ended in a dead end and that wasted a lot of our time. Marks were deducted in asking for directions, and our car had to ask for directions after coming back to the junction it had started from. Their car once turned 360 degrees at the junction and stopped on getting confused, they asked immediately, and were told the right direction, while we had lost a lot more time and had to do the same eventually.

Interviewer: Looks like we will get to see your driverless car fitted with a GPS map racing on our roads as part of your MS research!

Vivaan (*elated*): Wish that happens, Sir!

Interviewer: I have a simple problem at hand; please help me find a solution for it.

You have a few jars filled with sand, which is leaking through a little hole at the jar bottom. You can change the size of the jars as much as you want so their capacity changes. But you can change the size only in number multiples of a base unit. The smallest size that you can achieve is a jar which gets emptied in one time unit.

You have to do certain tasks for certain time periods, like a task should be done for 5 units of time, another for 12 units of time, etc.

For this purpose, you have to decide on the minimum number of jars you will need to use and their sizes so that you can easily find out any time durations.

(Interviewer: Believe me, this is a simple problem, the only complicated thing about it is its description.)

Vivaan: Please give me a few minutes, Sir.

Interviewer: Sure.

(Vivaan: All numbers are either multiples of two or three or multiple plus one. So if I take one jar of size 6, another of size 8 and a third one of size 9, I can count 1, 2, 3 with these combinations. But to find a number that is a multiple of 4 but not 3, it will be too complicated in this manner. Wait, to simplify, all numbers are multiples of 1 or are multiples of 2. So I should be able to do it using a jar of size 1 and size 2 only …)

Vivaan: Sir, we can find this out by using three jars, one of size 1 and the other two of size 2. The logic would be as follows:

Fill bigger jar with sand and let the leaking sand fill into the smaller jar. The time taken to fill the smaller jar would be one unit. Replace the smaller filled jar with the empty one. Transfer the contents of the first smaller jar to the bigger jar. When the second smaller jar fills, that will mark completion of second time unit. Now replace the second filled smaller jar with the first, now empty the smaller jar, and repeat the process to find any units of time as needed.

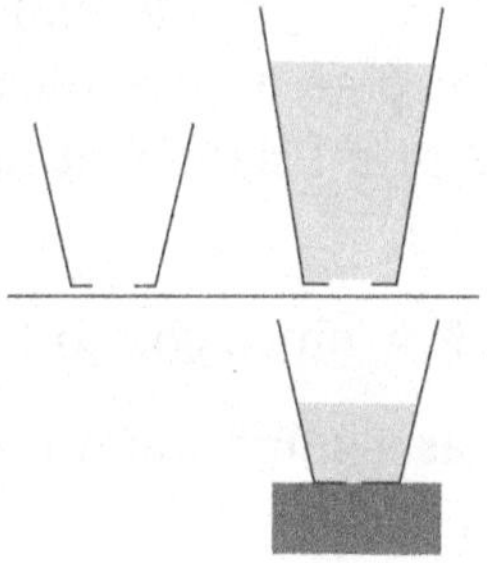

Interviewer: Can you write a C program to simulate this?

Vivaan: Yes, Sir. The code lines are as follows:

```
/*******************************************************/
#include <stdio.h>

void main()
{
```

```
        int x=1,y=2,n, i;
        printf("Enter the time unit\n");
        scanf("%d", &n);
        if (n==1)
                printf("%d \n", x);
        else if (n==2)
                printf("%d \n", y);
        else
        {
                printf("%d \n", y);
                for (i=1;i<=n-y;i++)
                        printf("%d \n",x);
        }
}
/***************************************************/
```

There are four variables in this program. y represents the bigger jar, x is one of the smaller jars, n is the total time duration, and i is the intermediate jar. If n < 3, we use one of the two jars to find the time directly. If n > 3, we use the bigger jar and keep on adding the smaller jar content to find the total time elapsed. The printf statements display the order in which the time units will be counted.

Interviewer: This is fine. How much comfortable are you with C?

Vivaan: Sir, we studied it as a subject and I am quite comfortable with it.

Interviewer: All right, look at this code and tell me the output:

```
/***************************************************/
struct s
{
        int i;
        struct s *p;
};
void main()
```

```
{
    struct s var1, var2;
    var1.i = 100;
    var2.i = 200;
    var1.p=&var2;
    var2.p=&var1;
    printf("\n%d %d", var1.p->i, var2.p -> i);
    printf("\n%u %u", var1.p, var2.p);
}
/*******************************************************/
```

Vivaan: This is a self-referential structure. Element i value for structure variable var1 is 100 and for var2 is 200.

Element structure pointer for structure variable var1 points to the structure variable var2 base address.

Element structure pointer for structure variable var2 points to the structure variable var1 base address.

Thus the first printf statement prints 200 100.

The second statement prints the address values. Suppose structure var1 begins at 1000 and var2 begins at 2000, then the values printed are 2000 1000.

Interviewer: If we add an argument var1.p + 1 in the second printf statement, then what will it print?

Vivaan: It would be 2000 1000 2004.

Interviewer: How did you arrive at 2004?

Vivaan: Sir, any pointer operation increments by units, not by mere integers. So an operation like "integer pointer + 1" increments the address value by 2 as the integer by size is 2. It points to the next valid location that can store a similar data type.

On the same lines, the size of the structure is 4 bytes, 2 for the integer variable and 2 for the pointer. Thus "+1" increments address by 4 bytes.

Interviewer: I understand that. What will happen if I make a small change in the structure definition?

```
struct s
{
    int i;
    struct s p;
};
```

Vivaan: The data type struct s is not fully defined till now, so it will not compile.

Interviewer: Please have a look at this program and explain the output.

```
/*****************************************************/
union
{
    int value;
    struct s
    {
        char first;
        char second;
    } test;
}number;
void main()
{
    number.value = 12345;
    printf("\n%d %d %d\n", number.value, number.test.first, number.test.
second);
}
/*****************************************************/
```

Vivaan: This is union. I don't remember it much but I will give it a try. The value for "number.value" is certainly the number 12345. What happens to structure "test"? It shares the address space with the integer variable value. Yes, I got it. We can store any one of the elements at a time in the union. As the integer is already stored, we can refer to its parts through the structure "test" elements.

The number is stored in hex format. Let's suppose the hex format for 12345 is 5123. Then number.test.first will refer to value 23 and number. test.second will refer to 51. Thus the printf statement output would be

```
12345 23 51
```

Interviewer: I must say you have got a good memory!

Vivaan: Thanks, Sir.

Interviewer: What is your final year project about?

Vivaan: Sir, we are trying to develop a mini search engine that can look up pictures on our intranet and return results. I would like to say that it is not going to be anywhere near to what Google is offering in terms of picture search, but we are trying to work out the algorithms so that we can at least pull pictures of interest from our intranet or our own computers. And it would be limited to searching images of the jpeg format.

Most of the picture search right now is about searching a file by its name, not by its content. But Google has introduced content-based search now. We are trying to do something similar there. We are using many of Google's concepts of search.

The first concept is about indexing. We are trying to create an index of all the jpg images available on the intranet. We are storing the image file location, name, image attributes like its pixel height and width, image header comments, and the type of image like grayscale or color. In addition to this, we are working on an algorithm to detect whether this is a line diagram or a captured photo. That information would also be stored in the index.

We are building an interface to accept the input search image.

From this uploaded image, we will extract the header attributes and match them against the indexes we have. In case a match is found, the next would be to match the data content of the uploaded image with the image referred by the index. If it matches, that will be returned as a result. If no match is found, the image with matching header will be returned with an alert that it is a probable match, not confirmed.

If the input and stored images are same in appearance, but have different resolutions, we won't be able to match those.

Interviewer: Which technology is being used to accomplish this and why?

Vivaan: Sir, we are using Java for the ease of GUI design and index creation. The matching algorithm could have been implemented in C also very easily, but then interface was an issue there. And I have got an opportunity to learn and work on Java also.

Interviewer: That's truly amazing. You are focused on building up your CV for MS. Have you started applying already?

Vivaan: Not yet, Sir; I don't think I will get calls from any good universities right now because of my engineering discipline. I would be applying after two years. In the meanwhile, I will be doing a distance learning postgraduate course in Computer Science along with my job.

(Interviewer: Oh boy, I don't know if you are telling truth or repeating a well-rehearsed reply to avoid the interview trap that tries to learn your intentions to join the company, but I will believe you. You want to know why? Because I have seen that it's the students actually planning for higher studies immediately who never mention a word about it during interviews. And here you are being so bindaas about it!)

Interviewer: You look all set! I am just wondering how your department teachers will react to your computer-based project.

Vivaan (*grinning*): We will upgrade that robotic car for better traction over slippery surfaces and for travel over bumpy surface and present that as our project.

Interviewer: Smart! Very smart! It was a very pleasant experience talking to you, Vivaan. Have a good day!

Vivaan: Thanks. Good day, Sir!

SCENE 3

The interviewer does not have an iota of doubt over selecting Vivaan. He is happy that the long day for him has started on such a good note. It takes him a couple of minutes to sign off his evaluation form.

Discipline Knowledge: Very Good

C – Very Good

Java – Good

Aptitude and Problem Solving – Very Good

Project Description – Very Good; has done a computer's project of his own in addition to curriculum requirements.

Achievements – Robotics contest prize winner at IIT.

Communication – Very Good

SCENE 4

On board their flight back, the five Newton Networks executives are discussing how each one of them ended up selecting one candidate each from this campus. As Vivaan's is the only non-CS student selected, everyone is curious about him and gets his interviewer talking about him.

"Based on my personal experience with non-CS-background freshers, I was hardly inclined at picking one, but this chap Vivaan literally forced me to select him. He is passionate about computers and IT and his knowledge shows that clearly. He wants to do an MS in Computer Science and is preparing well his CV for that. He has written some cool algorithms that got him a prize at IIT. He is pretty good at C and knows almost everything about it. Knows about concepts like fuzzy logic, cloud computing, etc. Even CS students don't understand stuff outside of their curriculum so well!

This does not mean that he has ignored his discipline. He is pretty good there also. He is doing a mechanical project for his curriculum and at the same time he is doing an image search implementation project in Java. And he has completed a good part of both the projects though he has more than a semester at his disposal.

Strong aptitude, good logic, good communication skills, good attitude, and a child-like curiosity are added bonuses.

Now tell me, don't you agree that he forced me to select him?"

* * *

9

BioTech's Raghu Discovers Himself at Swarm Analytics

SCENE 1

Raghu is happy that he could finally clear a GD round. This would be his first technical interview and he is sort of confident about it. He belongs to the first BioTech batch graduating from the institute. Lack of a godfather from his discipline is acutely felt by him. But there is no dearth of tips given, the most important one that biotech would be all Greek and Latin to IT interviewers. So he should focus on his achievements, strengths, and basics of computer programming. Another important tip has been that companies pay more attention to communication skills these days, so he has concentrated on improving his fluency this whole semester. And his efforts have paid off as he has cleared the GD.

SCENE 2

Raghu: Good evening, Sir! This is Raghu.

Interviewer: Hello Ravi, Good evening. Please take a seat.

Raghu: Thank you, Sir.

(The interviewer is going through his CV.)

Raghu: Sir, shall I give my introduction?

(Puzzled Interviewer: Don't bother. I have already read it all in your CV.)

Interviewer (*with a fake smile*): Yes please.

Raghu: Thank you, Sir. This is Raghu from the biotechnology department. We are the first BioTech batch passing out from this college. My father is a businessman and my younger sister is doing fashion designing. I know C language … my other interests are reading novels and watching movies.

Interviewer: You know C language … that's good. Look at these lines and give me the output.

```
/*************************************************************/
void main()
{
        int i = 3, j = 6;
        printf("%s \n", (i>(j%=i)?"False":"True"));
}
/*************************************************************/
```

Raghu: What will be the output … I think it will give compilation error.

Interviewer: Why?

Raghu: Sorry, Sir.

Interviewer: No problem; look at this program and tell me what would be the output

```
/*************************************************************/
void main()
{
        int i, j;
        for (; i<j, j>i;i+=i,j-=i) printf("\n I and J values are : %d %d \n", i, j);
}
/*************************************************************/
```

Raghu: Hmm … no initialization is done for the "for" loop … Sorry Sir, I am getting confused.

Interviewer: A number is given as input. Can you write a program to count the number of digits in it? It can have any number of digits 1, 2, 3, 15, anything.

Raghu: I will try.

```
/*************************************************************/
int number,i,j;
      printf("Enter a number \n");
      scanf("%d",&number);
      for (j=1; j<i; j++)
      {
             i = number;
number = number % 10;
      }
/*************************************************************/
```

Interviewer: You are sure this will work?

Raghu (*doubtful*): Yes … Sir …

Interviewer: What is this percentage sign that you have used?

Raghu: It is a modulus operator. It is used in digit-counting programs.

Interviewer (*smiling inwardly*): I see that! All right, I am writing 2 lines, tell me what they would do.

```
/*************************************************************/
for(j=0; number>0; j++)
{
      number=/10;
}
/*************************************************************/
```

Raghu: It will divide number by 10 and assign new value to number variable.

Interviewer: Why do you think the variable j has been used here?

Raghu: That is the for-loop counter, for that purpose.

(Interviewer: It is the digit counter, boy!)

Interviewer: Have you studied about databases?

Raghu: Yes, Sir.

Interviewer: What is the function served by foreign key constraints in a database?

Raghu: Foreign keys are used for referring to master data.

Interviewer: See we have these three tables: Table A, Table B, and Table C.

Between Tables A and B, Table A is the master table. DEPT_CD is the foreign key field that is being referred to by Table B.

Between Tables B and C, Table B is the master table. STUDENT_ID is the foreign key field that is being referred to by Table C.

What will happen if we delete the row with STUDENT_ID value "4" from Table B?

Table A

DEPT_ID	DEPT_CD
1	CS
2	BT

Table A —DEPT_CD→ Table B

Table B

DEPT_CD	STUDENT_ID
CS	1
CS	2
BT	3
CS	4
BT	5
BT	6

Table B —STUDENT_ID→ Table C

Table C

STUDENT_ID	ELECTIVE_CD
1	STAT
1	AINT
2	AINT
2	NNET
3	STAT
3	NNET
4	AINT
4	NNET
5	STAT
6	AINT

Raghu: Sorry Sir, can you please repeat the question?

Interviewer: Why not? I want to know if we delete the row with STUDENT_ID value "4" from Table B, then what will happen to the Table A and Table C data as some foreign key constraints are involved?

Raghu: Table C rows with STUDENT_ID 4 will be automatically deleted. Not sure about Table A; there is no row with value "4" there.

(Interviewer: If you had simply said no row will be deleted from Table A, I would have been fooled into thinking that you understand this concept.)

Interviewer: What should I do if I don't want Table C rows to be automatically deleted?

Raghu: I don't know that much Sir.

Interviewer: Do you know about cascading?

Raghu: No Sir ...

Interviewer: OK, let's talk about biotech then. Tell me about your project.

(Raghu: Project! What to tell about that, it is not even finalized! Let me tell about a minor project.)

Raghu: Project ... hmm ... it is about enzyme study in our lab.

Interviewer: Tell me more about it.

Raghu: We have made a setup to monitor enzyme activity under changing temperature, pH, and pressure conditions. It is known that enzymes need a very stable environment for their function, but our guide has asked us to analyze the relationship between environment change and activity level.

Interviewer: I want more specific details. Which enzymes are you using for this study? What is the temperature and pressure range for this? Which substrates are you using to determine the activity?

Raghu: We have used enzymes called cellulases, and the substrate is rotting wood. Don't remember the range used but we have noted down all the findings.

(Interviewer: Let me test if you even know what you are blabbering!)

Interviewer: Why do cows ruminate?

Raghu: To digest their food properly.

Interviewer: I mean why they can't eat it properly the first time like dogs and cats do?

Raghu: Not sure, Sir.

(Interviewer: Have you really done a project on cellulase? I am surprised you couldn't even tell that cellulase is supplied by microorganisms in the cow's rumen to digest grass.)

Interviewer: No problem. What is ajinomoto chemically and what is the chemical used in the artificial sweeteners?

Raghu: Ajinomoto is a salt, monosodium glutamate. Aspartame is used as the sweetener.

Interviewer: What is Bt Brinjal and what is the debate around it?

Raghu: Sir, Bt Brinjal is Bacillus thuringiensis brinjal; BT is a soil microbe. A gene from the bacteria, Cry1Ac," is inserted into the Brinjal DNA. This gene is considered toxic for insects and is supposed to make the plant naturally resistant. There is debate on the safety of this gene for human consumption. There is also fear of good insects like butterflies being badly affected by it.

Interviewer: You came prepared for this question, isn't it?

Raghu (*smiling*): Yes, Sir.

Interviewer: It's good to prepare. What are HeLa cells?

Raghu: Hella cells ... Hella ... HeLa cells, yes, they keep on dividing and do not die after a certain time. They are used in biomedical research.

(Interviewer: It is a tragic irony that Henrietta's cells which refuse to die and are keeping people around the world alive killed her.)

Interviewer: What is so special about them?

Raghu: They have more chromosomes and the telomerase sequence is somewhat changed in these cells.

Interviewer: Do you have any idea about the Nobel prize being conferred for telomerase?

Raghu: No, Sir.

Interviewer: Try to recollect; it has happened recently while you were here in this institute.

Raghu: Yes, Sir, yes, for telomere discovery.

Interviewer: The Nobel prize was conferred more for the impact of the discovery on cancer research! Anyways, what are telomeres?

Raghu: They are present at chromosome end. They prevent DNA shortening.

Interviewer: How?

Raghu: Sorry, Sir, I don't remember.

Interviewer: Which strand is shortened otherwise, lagging or leading?

Raghu: I think leading one ...

Interviewer: What do you understand by X linkage or crisscross inheritance?

Raghu: Sorry ... Sir ...

Interviewer: Then tell me something about ribosome?

Raghu: It is used in protein synthesis ... Sorry Sir, don't remember much on it ... we studied cell structure in first sem ...

Interviewer: I will give a hint; another Nobel prize has been awarded for it recently.

Raghu: Nobel Prize ... for ribosome ...

Interviewer: List any two techniques used for selecting a sample for a study, for example, a sample for clinical trials of drugs?

Raghu: Not sure, Sir ...

Interviewer: Do you know about the open source drug discovery project done on TB bacterium recently and the controversy surrounding it?

Raghu: No, Sir.

(Interviewer: I was thinking that you must have participated in it!)

Interviewer: No problem. Let's talk about something else. What are your future plans? For how long do you plan to work with us?

Raghu: Sir, I want to work at your company for 20-25 years. After that I will start my own venture.

Interviewer: Why so long? Why don't you start right away?

Raghu: I need experience.

Interviewer: 10 years is a decent enough experience in that case, why 25 then?

Raghu: Then I will learn and maybe in 10 years then.

Interviewer: And suppose you learn that we are not a good company in 5 years, then?

Raghu: Company is good, Sir.

Interviewer: Company policies change and it becomes very bad in 2 years?

Raghu: Everybody will leave then. But I am sure that won't happen in 2 years also.

(Interviewer: So I see you are down from 20 years commitment to 2 years within 2 minutes; interesting, very interesting.)

Interviewer: As last question, I give you complete choice. Tell me about any thing technical, anything that you know and came prepared for.

Raghu (*confident*): Sir, I know about Bioinformatics. It is about integrating biotechnology and computer science. Scientists are doing more and more research taking help of computers to understand data. DNA fingerprinting being done in forensic labs is an example. Analyzing fossils to understand evolution of species is another example.

Interviewer: Very good; do you have any questions?

Raghu: Yes, Sir; I want to ask how do you know about biotechnology. I was told that IT people don't have that background.

Interviewer: Very good question and I know it is not necessary for me to answer that. But I will answer that: I have done M.Sc. in Biology! And I had looked at your college site to get an idea of the syllabus as it was the first batch, so I know that I asked you nothing that you were not supposed to study! And many of them were about general awareness.

Since you have asked this, I have one more question for you now. You did not revise your subjects at all for this interview?

Raghu: Sorry, Sir, I thought only computer questions would be asked.

Interviewer: Are you sure of that? You could not even answer the computer questions I tried to ask you initially.

Raghu: Not programs, Sir, I mean questions like what is the difference between a while and do-while loop.

Interviewer: I understand it now! You came prepared for a theoretical round. Do you now understand what you have to keep in mind for future interviews?

Raghu: Yes, Sir, thanks so much for your time.

SCENE 3

The interviewer dejectedly completes the mandatory feedback ritual

Discipline Knowledge - Not Acceptable

C Basics – Not Acceptable

Aptitude – Poor

Communication – Acceptable

Attitude – Frank and straightforward

SCENE 4

The interviewer is feeling depressed. He had not yet met any student as hopeless as Raghu. He tries to analyze the discussion he had some time back.

One remarkable quality about Raghu is that he is confident, he knew he did not know most of the answers, but he was quite casual about it ... wait, shall I call that overconfidence? God knows!

If he is really serious about a job and is not thinking of joining his father next year, then he must have been disillusioned today. How could he think that no one is going to ask him a word about his discipline! Interviewers might not have studied everything from books, but there is no dearth of information on all fields in the media today. He thought only Bt Brinjal would be known to all and came prepared to answer that including the gene name but did not know much about DNA replication and telomeres! Worse, he did not remember ribosomes; come on, scientist V. Ramakrishnan's achievement was so hugely publicized by our media. I can't believe he could clear seven semesters' papers!

And who learns C definitions by heart? He aspires to join us with such pathetic programming skills! On top of that he mentions knowledge of C in his introduction. I think he should practice writing simple lines of code for a few months to get started.

He is also very weak in aptitude, cannot correlate anything; imagine, he spoke of Bioinformatics but is blissfully unaware of the TB OSDD project which is yet to be included in his textbooks.

He sounds quite convincing when he talks about things he knows or remembers. But that alone won't be enough for me! What matters most is that he is bad at even simple programs and lacks an understanding of most of his subject areas. And that is good enough justification for me not to recommend him for the next round.

* * *

10

IT's Tejaswi is Picked by ARAASIN

SCENE 1

ARAASIN's campus visit announcement just three days before the commencement of vacations has taken everyone by surprise. Tejaswi has her tickets booked for the day-after-tomorrow flight for attending her parents' silver jubilee anniversary celebrations. As the GD results and interview slots are announced, she is crestfallen to see that she has been placed in the last slot and she might have to miss the party. She presents her case before the placement department and is bluntly told that her request for an earlier slot can be put up before ARAASIN executives, but the final decision would be theirs and the placement department won't be able to help on that. She has almost lost all hopes when the happy news is conveyed to her that she will be called within thirty minutes for her interview. In the heart of her heart, she is apprehensive that an interview completed in a hurry toward the end of the day might ruin her chances of being selected. But what could be done now? She has already gone ahead and taken the risk.

SCENE 2

Interviewer: Hi Tejaswi, good evening, or should I say good night!

Tejaswi: Hi M'am, very good evening. Thank you so much for agreeing to take my interview now. I am so sorry, I am holding you here.

Interviewer: My pleasure, Tejaswi! Don't worry about that, I had to wait for my colleagues anyways and they are not going to get free any time soon.

Tejaswi: Thank you, M'am.

Interviewer: You're welcome! Tell me, if we had not agreed to pre-pone your interview slot, what would you have done, stayed behind or left?

Tejaswi: M'am, ARAASIN is an employee-friendly company and has received the Best Employer of the Year Award. I was hopeful that my request would be considered …

Interviewer: Let's forget about that right now. Just tell me what you would have done!

Tejaswi: I would have gone home, M'am, as this occasion is very important.

Interviewer: So that means ARAASIN is less important for you; basically, you are not interested!

Tejaswi: M'am, it is not like this. Our seniors at ARAASIN are all praise for the company and it is given the 'dream company' tag also. I would have certainly appeared for its off-campus event in that case.

Interviewer: All right! What are your favorite subjects?

Tejaswi: M'am, my favorite subjects are networking, databases, and programming languages, especially Java …

Interviewer: Tell me as many possible differences as you can between C and Java that you have encountered while programming till now?

Tejaswi:

1. The very first difference is that Java is object oriented; all code has to be enclosed within classes there. C is a procedural language without the object concept. So we write more functions to modularize code in C.
2. In Java, we can write code in the order we desire. In C, we have to declare all the variables first in the type declaration and initialization block before the start of any executable statement but Java has no such constraint. This is very useful when writing big programs. We can declare a variable just before we need to use that – no need to go back to the declaration block to add it.
3. Another very noticeable difference is in the name of the code file. We can name a C program file in the manner we please irrespective of the function names being used inside but a Java class file should be named same as the class defined inside.

4. Data types are also handled differently. For example, C integers are 2 bytes while Java primitive data type int is 32 bits long. This makes it really convenient to handle most of the looping logic using integers in Java without worrying about going beyond range.
5. C does no bound checking for arrays: we have to be careful about going beyond the defined size, but Java throws ArrayIndexOutOfBoundsException.
6. C uses pointer concept to implement call by reference and, as programmers, we need to make use of this concept. Java has removed the use of pointers by programmers. It inherently handles address allocation. Through the use of keyword "new," it takes care of dynamic memory allocation at run time. A new object variable is assigned the address of the object instance but C-type pointer arithmetic is not supported on this variable. That has in fact made Java very secure.
7. Call by reference is also very simple in Java as the object variable stores a reference to the object, not the actual value.
8. C code is compiled into object code which is platform dependent and is not portable, for example, between Windows and Linux. Java code is interpreted into Bytecode. Bytecode is portable and is executed by JVM.
9. We can do exception handling in Java, which is not possible in C.
10. Method overloading is also supported by Java and not C.
11. Another difference is in memory management. In C, the programmer has to take the responsibility for freeing up memory. I have read that this leads to memory leak problem in C programs, if not handled properly. Java uses automatic garbage collection for this purpose, which frees up the memory used by any object that is not referenced anymore.
12. And M'am, I really miss scanf's equivalent in Java. Console input looks a very big task for the simple Java programs we run for learning purpose.

Interviewer: That was a very comprehensive list! What will happen if you define more than one class in the same program file?

Tejaswi: M'am, in that case, multiple object files will be created during compilation. A separate .class file will be created for each of the classes defined in the single .java file.

Interviewer: What will happen if you try to compile the following program written in file Sub.java?

```
/*****************************************************/
class sub
{
	public static void main(String[] args)
	{
		System.out.println("Hello, You are in Sub Class!");
		sub1 stest = new sub1();
		stest.check();
	}

	class sub1
	{
		void check()
		{
			System.out.println("Void Check, you are in Sub1 Class!");
		}
	}
}
/*****************************************************/
```

Tejaswi: It should create two class files Sub.class and sub1.class but I am not sure as the sub1 class is nested.

Interviewer: I think it won't compile! I am curious what have you read about memory leak?

Tejaswi: M'am, it is like this: You run some code which has a big loop and inside the loop some memory is allotted at run time. The loop completes but this memory is not freed. In the next iteration, some more memory will be allotted. If it is an infinite loop or a very big loop, a lot of system memory will be blocked by the small program even though it is not being used for any purpose. We can actually see the available physical memory being reduced in the Task Manager. It happens a lot of times when we work on Turbo C; we see that the system hangs and cannot accept even a single click. Then we reboot the system and it works fine.

Interviewer (*impressed*): I am pleasantly surprised to hear your beautiful explanation as students hardly ever mention this term. Now, can you please write a program to implement a queue through Java? The code should accept the queue size as input, that is, the queue size should be dynamic.

Tejaswi: Yes, M'am. I have done this for stack, so I will try to do the same for a queue.

```
/****************************************************/
//SECTION HEADER
import java.util.Scanner;

class ClassQueue
{
        private int i;
        private int q[];
        private int tail;

/****************************************************/

//SECTION CONSTRUCTOR
        ClassQueue(int size)
        {
                i = /*--size;*/ size - 1;
                q  = new int[size];
                tail = -1;
        }

/****************************************************/

//SECTION QUEUE SETUP
        void insert(int item)
        {
                if(tail==i)
```

```
                System.out.println("Queue is full, please wait");
            else
                q[++tail] = item;
        }

/**************************************************************/

//SECTION QUEUE ITEM RETRIEVE

        int remove()
        {
            if (tail < 0)
            {
                System.out.println("Queue is empty, place a request now");
                return -1;
            }
            else
                /*return([i-tail--]);*/ return(q[i-tail--]);
        }
}

/**************************************************************/

//SECTION MAIN
class QueueUse
{
        public static void main(String args[])
        {
            System.out.println("Enter Queue Size");
            Scanner in = new Scanner(System.in);
            int size = in.nextInt();
            System.out.println("Number read " + size);
            ClassQueue Queue1 = new ClassQueue(size);

            for (int i=0; i<size; i++)
```

```
                Queue1.insert(i);
            for (int i=0; i<size; i++)
                System.out.println(Queue1.remove());
        }
}

/**************************************************/
```

Interviewer: The code size looks impressive! Please explain it to me.

(Tejaswi: Am I really that good or is it that M'am is generous with compliments? I was hardly expecting to hear such nice things during an interview!)

Tejaswi: M'am, I will start from the main section to explain this code. I am trying to read the queue size using the Scanner class. It is available in the java.util package. I am using the Scanner constructor that accepts InputStream type argument, and System.in is an object of this type. Method nextInt() reads the input and returns it as an integer, which is being assigned to our regular variable size. In the statement

ClassQueue Queue1 = new ClassQueue(size);

a new instance of the class ClassQueue is created and its reference is assigned to the object variable Queue1. We are also initializing this instance by passing the queue size to the constructor ClassQueue().

Interviewer: Let's go to the header section now.

Tejaswi: Here I am using three variables. Array q is the actual queue to hold the values. Variable i will be used to refer to the queue size and variable tail will refer to the last item in the queue at any time, beyond which the queue is empty.

Interviewer: Why have you defined them as private variables?

Tejaswi: These variables are defined as private so that they cannot be directly accessed by any other class.

Interviewer: Let's have a quick look at the constructor section now. What is happening here?

Tejaswi: M'am, the class variables are being initialized here. Suppose I entered a value of 10 which was stored in the size variable. Now the upper index of this array should be 9. So assign a value 1 less than the size to the variable i.

The array for queue, q, is assigned the size value 10.

M'am, I made a mistake there … we should not decrement the size while assigning to i. Instead it should be written as

i = size -1.

The current position for the queue last item is set to -1.

Interviewer: I think I can understand the queue setup logic. Let's talk about the retrieval logic.

Tejaswi: M'am, if the queue is empty, then the variable tail has a value -1 and the print statement message is displayed.

Otherwise, we have to read the value that is logically at the zeroth position.

Interviewer: What is logical zero position; can't we use q[0] directly?

Tejaswi: We cannot use q[0] directly as we are never shifting data in the array as happens in a real queue. If we see this logic for a small array with five elements, as elements start getting removed from the queue, we need to consider the next higher element as the queue head. That is nothing but equal to "i – tail." Keeping the data fields physical position unchanged, we can save a lot of compare and swap operations.

Array Elements	A	B	C	D	E
Physical Index Position	0	1	2	3	4
Logical Index Position after removing first element	Null	0	1	2	3
Logical Index Position after removing second element	Null	Null	0	1	2
Logical Index Derivation	Array Max Index – Current Tail Position				

I missed the array name here. It should be

return(q[i-tail––]); instead of return([i-tail––]);

Interviewer: Really good job, Tejaswi! I have few code snippets for you. Have a look at the first one and tell me what will happen.

Tejaswi: The first program will not compile.

```
/*****************************************************/
class Array
{
	public static void main(String[] args)
	{
		int[2] arr;
		arr[0] = 1; arr[1] = 2;
		System.out.println("Array values are :" + arr[0] + " " + arr[1]);
	}
}
/*****************************************************/
```

Interviewer: What makes you say so?

Tejaswi: This is C style of array declaration. Java array declaration is different as it is dynamic in nature. We need to write int[] arr = new int[2] so that memory is allocated for this array object variable "arr." Alternatively, we can initialize the array as int[] arr = {1,2}.

Interviewer: How about the second program?

```
/*****************************************************/
class Mod
{
	public static void main(String[] args)
	{
		int x = 17;
		System.out.println("Remainder is :" + x % 5.5);
	}
}
/*****************************************************/
```

Tejaswi: M'am, it will print 0.5. Java promotes the expression to largest datatype. 5.5 is a double, so the expression "x % 5.5" returns a result of type double.

Interviewer: What would be the output of this program?

```
/*************************************************/

class Operator
{
    public static void main(String[] args)
    {
        int z = 4;
        int a = 0;
        if (a == 0 && z/++a < 2 & ++a < 0)
            System.out.println("True " + a);
        else
            System.out.println("False "  + a);
    }
}

/*************************************************/
```

Tejaswi: M'am, the expression in the if condition will be parsed as per the precedence rule. The unary operators are the highest in order, so "a" is incremented twice and it becomes 2. Then the division takes place. So the expression becomes

(a == 0 && 2 < 2 & 2 < 0)

After that, comparisons are done. So the expression now becomes

(false && false & false)

I have got confused which of these two will be evaluated first, but the result for this will always be false.

Interviewer: I have an array of strings. Can you please write a piece of code to display the length and content of the individual strings using a "foreach" loop?

Tejaswi: M'am, can you please explain it a little more?

Interviewer: Sure. For example, I have four names stored in an array format:

"Coleridge"

"Leonardo"

"Albert"

"Isaac"

I want to see the length and the value for each of these strings.

Tejaswi: Thanks, M'am, I got it. I will write down the code for this.

```
/*****************************************************/
class Str
{
        public static void main(String args[])
        {
                String[] list = {"Coleridge", "Leonardo", "Albert", "Isaac"};
                for (String name : list )
                System.out.println("Length : " + name.length() + " Name is : " +
name );
        }
}
/*****************************************************/
```

Interviewer: This one looks short and sweet! Please explain what's going on inside the main().

Tejaswi: M'am, first of all, we are creating an array of string objects and calling this as "list."

Then we are reading the elements of this array one by one using the for loop. This version of for loop is supported by Java. As the list array elements are of type string, we are using the variable name of type string in the for loop. The list array elements from index position 0 till last are automatically referenced.

String.length() method gives the length of the string and that is used in the print statement.

Interviewer: Now I don't want to initialize the list in the program but rather pass it at run time through command line. Please make changes in the code for this.

Tejaswi: For this, we can comment out the first line.

```
//String[] list = {"Coleridge", "Leonardo", "Albert", "Isaac"};
```

And the second line changes as:

for (String name : ~~list~~args)

Interviewer: What is "args"?

Tejaswi: It is the argument string passed to the main function. It is being defined as an array of strings, so that each of the arguments gets stored as an element of the array args[]. So args[] will behave the same as list[] from the previous code.

Interviewer: All right, Tejaswi. Any idea what will happen if I write main(String test[]).

Tejaswi: M'am ... I am not sure if we need to use the name as "args" only, never tried it like this.

Interviewer: Name doesn't matter, Tejaswi. Test[] will work just as fine as args[].

Tejaswi: OK, M'am.

Interviewer: Consider another situation now. You have a pre-sorted array with n, say 1000, numbers. You have to search for the presence of a particular number in this array. Please write a program to do so.

Tejaswi: Please give me few minutes, M'am.

(Tejaswi: The array is sorted; so a normal array scan won't be good, need to go for a binary search for this one. The logic would be to divide the array into two parts and select the part the number might belong to and then repeat this process, considering the selected part as a new array.)

Tejaswi: M'am, can I use the binarySearch() function directly?

Interviewer: You mean from the Arrays class?

Tejaswi: Yes, M'am.

Interviewer: It's good to see that you have the knowledge of inbuilt classes, but at this moment it would be good if you could write down your own logic for this.

Tejaswi: Sure, M'am, I will write down the code for this one.

```
/*********************************************************/
class Searchl
{
    public static void main (String [] args)
    {
        int number = Integer.parselnt(args [0]) ; // Read Number
        int lower=0, upper, mid; // Array Search variables
      boolean notfound = true;
       int[] list = {2,4,6,8,10,12,14,16,18,20}; //Sample Array
      upper = list.length; //Upper points to Array Top
        while(lower < upper & notfound) //Till the entire array is covered
         {
           mid = (lower + upper) / 2; //Find current array section mid point
           if (number < list [mid]) -upper = mid; //Select the lower half of current array
          else if (number > list [mid]) lower = mid + 1; //Select the upper half of current
           else
           {
              System.out.println ("number" + number + "found at index" + mid);
              notfound = false;
           }
         }
        if (notfound) System.out,println("Number" + number + "not found!");
```

```
    }
}
/*********************************************************************/
```

(The interviewer is keenly looking at the code as Tejaswi is writing it down.)

Interviewer: This is quite self-explanatory! I think you had mentioned something about method overloading support in Java. What is that?

Tejaswi: Method overloading is polymorphism. Method overloading happens when we create multiple methods with the same name in one class. All these methods have different number and types of parameters. I will take area method as an example.

```
double area(int i) { return 3.14 * i * i ; }
double area(int i, int j) { return i * j ; }
```

If we define both of these methods in one class, then "area" will be called as an overloaded method. One of these will be called at run time, depending on the number of arguments passed.

(The interviewer is informed by one of her colleagues that the team would be waiting for her in the GD room. She realizes that it has been a long discussion with Tejaswi.)

Interviewer: Very good, Tejaswi! I believe you would be at home this time tomorrow.

Tejaswi (*with a big smile*): Yes, yes, M'am, I will be at home.

Interviewer: So what are you gifting your parents?

Tejaswi: I have designed an album …

Interviewer: Hmm, personal touch! Nice, very nice! I will let you go then. Good night, Tejaswi!

Tejaswi: Thank you, M'am. Good night!

SCENE 3

As the interviewer hurriedly marks Tejaswi as a Tech Select, her friends are curious to know how things went for her. Tejaswi happily tells them that her interview started from Java and ended on Java, an area that she has been practicing religiously for the last 3 months. She feels quite relieved that she was not probed on Communication Systems and Microprocessors. And she is thankful to her friend for helping her prepare for the most expected question regarding her dilemma.

SCENE 4

The interview team lead calls the interviewer the next day.

Lead: I want to know the reasons for Tejaswi's selection as her marks are almost on border line and you have left her feedback form mostly blank.

Interviewer: I missed filling in the form properly as it had got quite late yesterday; I will do that now. The reason for her selection is straightforward. She is very good at communication, aptitude, and programming.

Lead: That's good then. But I am surprised you spoke so less about her!

Interviewer: I thought you might be busy, that's why thought of sparing you my analysis of hers, but I will do it now!

Tejaswi is endowed with a strong aptitude; the logic used by her reflects it amply. I asked her lots of questions on her favorite subject, Java, and gave her a lot of problems, and she could really solve all of them. I had made up my mind to pick her up by the way she explained the differences between C and Java. Even after being made a little nervous, she paid full attention to the question when I asked to list differences by her experience of using the two languages. And what she spoke is not the usual theoretical stuff found on Google for the differences. You could see the she had really done what she was explaining. And the fact that she could write almost error-free code, not even missing curly braces, on a piece of paper is a big proof that she has a lot of hands-on experience. I don't care how good or bad she is at other subjects. Given her do-it attitude and aptitude, she can pick up any technology coming her way.

Lead: Well, you have convinced me quite well! Tejaswi is definitely on board ARAASIN.

***

11

BioTech's Sourav has a Field Day at Pluto Computers

SCENE 1

Sourav is confident of getting through the first company that would allow biotech students to appear. At the moment, he is confused between IT and biotech career profiles. He likes both the domains and feels equally comfortable in both. While preparing for the interview a day before, he decides to choose IT over biotech, at least for the interview's sake. On the day of the interview, he has fully set himself to the IT mode.

SCENE 2

Sourav (*smartly*): Good morning, Sir!

Interviewer: Good morning, Sourav! How are you doing?

Sourav: I am fine, Sir. Thank you!

(Sourav's prim appearance and confident aura do not escape the interviewer's notice and create a favorable impression on him and raises his expectations from the interview too.)

Interviewer: Tell me something about yourself, Sourav.

Sourav: Sir, I am Sourav and I am pursuing BTech in BioTechnology. I have scored 8.5 CGPA till seventh semester. Biotechnology and computers are my interest areas. I have a good knowledge of C, data structures, and DBMS. I like writing articles on various subjects and I am a member of the college newsletter team. I am looking forward to start my career with a reputed IT firm like Pluto Computers.

Interviewer: You are on the newsletter team; you must be a well-known face on the campus in that case!

Sourav: Yes, Sir, many people read my articles and I get to interact with a lot of students for it also.

Interviewer (*smiling*): Have you already planned to write a piece on this interview experience?

Sourav (*smiling*): Hmm ... I had not thought about that till now but it is a good idea! Thanks, Sir.

Interviewer: You are welcome! Before we proceed further with this interview, I want you to know that I had got very excited on learning that I will be talking to a biotechnologist. I have many small curiosities and doubts related to this field. Do you mind if I bother you to get those clarified as a part of this discussion?

Sourav: No, Sir, I would be happy to explain.

Interviewer: Thanks, Sourav! And I hope you would not take me for a ride by just saying anything in case you also don't know.

Sourav (*smiling*): No, Sir, I promise!

(Interviewer: I hope you keep your promise because if you break it, I would know immediately and that would be very bad for you.)

Interviewer (*grateful*): Thank you very much! We have been calling AB as the sucker and O as the universal donor. But I recently learnt about an astonishing fact that it is just the reverse when it comes to plasma transfusion! Why so, any idea?

Sourav: Yes, Sir, it depends on the type of antibodies present in the blood plasma. When a person has a blood group AB, it means that his RBCs contain proteins or antigens A and B on their surface. His blood plasma lacks the IgM antibodies against both of these antigens.

A person with blood group O has no antigens on RBC surface and his blood plasma contains IgM antibodies against antigens A and B.

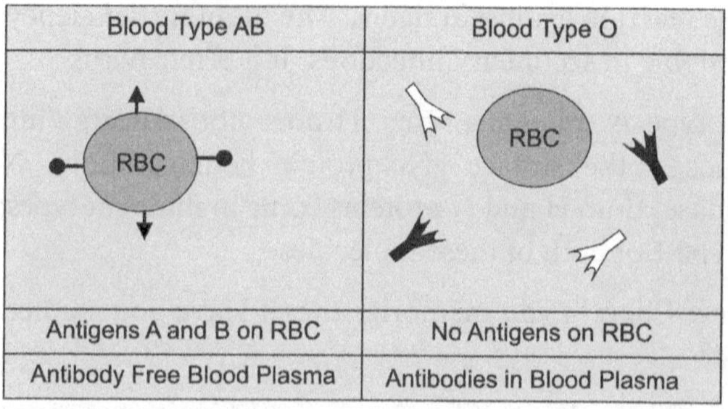

When RBCs from type O blood are transfused into AB-type blood, no immune reaction takes place as AB-type blood has no antibodies. But if plasma is transferred from an O-type person to AB-type person, the plasma antibodies will start attacking the AB-type RBCs that have the A and B antigens. That's why plasma of an O-type person cannot be transferred to an AB-type person.

But if plasma of AB type is transferred to an O-type person, then no immune reaction will take place as it is protein free.

This is how it happens for the other blood groups also.

Interviewer: OK, Sourav! What is this much talked about Oilzapper technology?

Sourav: Sir, it is an innovation for oil sludge bioremediation. It is a combination of five bacterial strains, each of which is capable of breaking down a component of crude oil into water and CO_2. It is being used by all major oil companies in our country now for reclaiming affected farmlands.

Interviewer: That is really cool; microbes are doing more good work for us nowadays. On the other hand, we get to read about too many viruses also, HPV, HIV-1, H1N1/A, all starting with an H! Can you please help me understand these mystery names?

Sourav: Yes Sir. HPV is the human papilloma virus and its various types are responsible for various cancer types in human. HPV types 16, 18, 45, and 31 are most commonly known as the most common cause for cervical cancer, the one that had afflicted late Jade Goody.

HIV is the human immune deficiency virus responsible for AIDS. It targets and eliminates T helper cells, which are responsible for signaling the immune reaction against antigens. The immune deficiency makes the body susceptible to secondary infections. It is a retrovirus.

H1N1 is a type A influenza virus. H does not indicate "human" here but it indicates the surface glycoprotein hemagglutinin. N indicates neuraminidase. Both H and N proteins come in different types; number 1 indicates type 1 of both of these molecules.

Interviewer: I hope I can memorize these! Have you studied about the ELISA test?

Sourav: Yes Sir, we have. It is enzyme-linked immunosorbent assay.

Interviewer: What sort of a test is that? The acronym sounded quite interesting but this expansion sounded complicated!

Sourav: This test is also based on the activity between antibodies and specific antigens and is used to detect the presence of antibodies in a test sample. A specific antigen is fixed on a plate and the test sample is added to this plate. Antibodies present, if any, bind with the antigen on the plate. The plate is washed to remove unbound items. Then an enzyme is added to attach to the bound antibodies. Unbound particles are again washed off. Finally a substrate is added to detect the bound enzyme.

As the binding and detection could take place if the correct antibody was present in the test sample, a positive response on substrate addition confirms the antibody presence.

Interviewer: All right. What is a retrovirus by the way?

Sourav: Normally, DNA contains the genetic material, and genetic information flows from DNA to RNA to proteins. Retroviruses are a special group of virus that contain genetic material in the form of RNA and can synthesize DNA from RNA. Reverse transcriptase is the enzyme used in the reverse process. Then this viral DNA integrates into host DNA to start the normal route of transcription and protein synthesis.

Interviewer: Integration with host DNA sounds somewhat similar to genetic engineering that is being done for GM crops, isn't it?

Sourav: Yes, Sir, it is similar in the respect that the final or the recombinant DNA consists of the host genes and the newly integrated genes. But genetic engineering done in lab is an elaborate process.

Interviewer: Please tell me more about this elaborate process.

Sourav: Sir, genetic engineering or recombinant DNA technology is very similar to a cut, paste, and copy operation that we follow for our assignment programs. A base program is built; then we search for an external function code that fulfills our requirements and has matching variables, for example, a function for finding prime numbers recursively. This function is cut and inserted at the correct place in the base program. This recombined program is compiled and tested. Finally, it is copied by the entire class and mailed to the lecturer individually.

Now, I will write down these computer operations and their equivalent operations from rDNA tech to explain how this technology works.

Computer Tech	Computer Process	rDNA Tech	rDNA process (relies heavily on enzymes)
Base program	Prepare code skeleton	Plasmid	Extract from bacterium like *E. coli*
Other program	Search for required function	Foreign DNA strand	Find a DNA strand with a required gene, for example, insulin-producing gene or insect toxicity gene
Prime function	Cut and the value is saved in memory	Useful DNA fragment	Cut with restriction endonucleases like EcoRI to form sticky ends
Merge programs	Copy at right place, match variables, call function	Recombine DNA	Base pairing at sticky ends through hydrogen bonds and DNA ligase induced fragments' annealing or phosphodiester covalent bonding
Final program	Compile and run	Recombined plasmid	Plasmid put back into bacterium (transformation)
Class copies	Copy through pen drive or mail	Engineered DNA clones	Bacterium clones or PCR
Submission	Mail assignment to the lecturer	rDNA Purification	Chromatography and precipitation

Interviewer: That's quite an interesting analogy, I must say! Did you think of it right now?

Sourav: No Sir, I summarized our subject, rDNA technology, like this while studying, as it involved too many parameters and too many names and we happened to study data structures also in the same semester.

(Interviewer: This chap is looking for ways to redirect the discussion toward computers but I am not complaining.)

Interviewer: Hmm, data structures … how did you find the subject?

Sourav: I found it an interesting subject.

Interviewer: Please write down the algorithm for a breadth-first search for a graph traversal.

Sourav: The BFS is implemented through a queue.

1. Each node is assigned an initial status value 1; this indicates ready state of the node.
2. The starting node A is put into the queue and its status is changed to 2, that is, waiting state.
3. The front node N of the queue is removed, processed, that is, compared or passed to some function as needed, and its status is changed to 3, i.e., processed.
4. From left to right, all the neighbors of N that are still in ready state are added to the queue and their status is changed to waiting state.
5. Then steps 3 and 4 are repeated until the queue gets empty.

Interviewer: Look at the following graph and tell me the order in which the nodes will be traversed during a BFS.

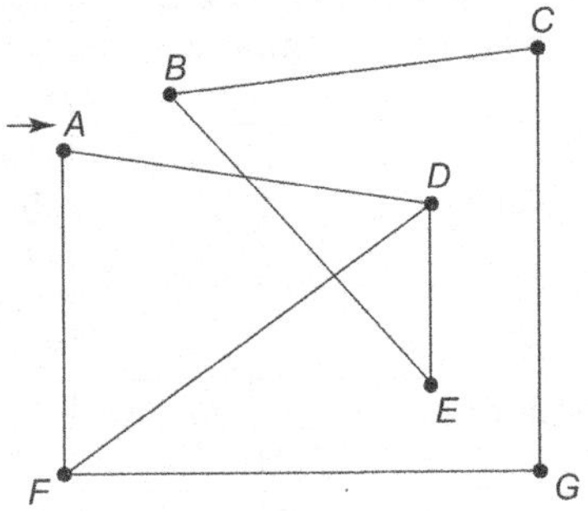

Sourav: Sir, I will use this legend to mark the node status and store the traversed node in the queue. Starting with the A node,

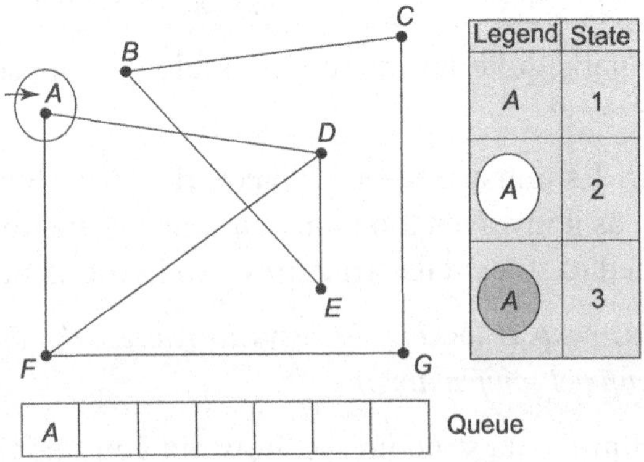

Proceeding as follows to neighboring nodes,

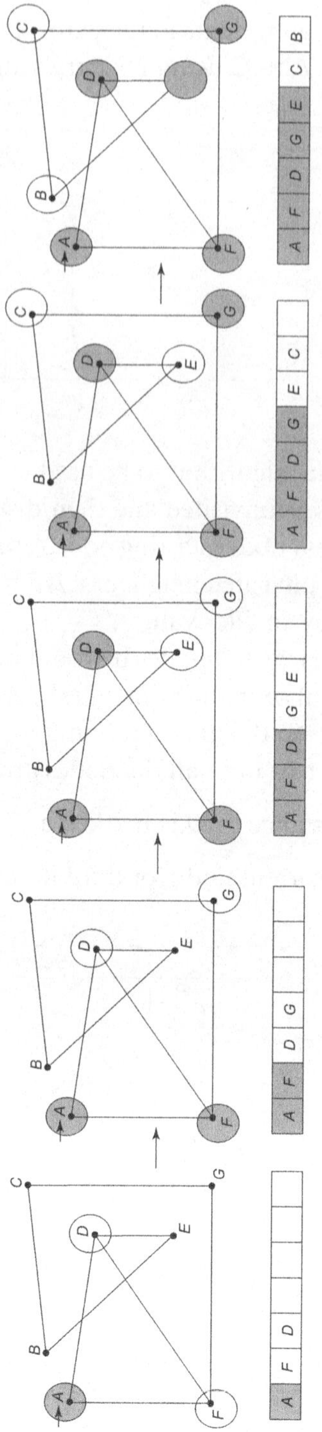

the order of traversal would be AFDGECB.

Interviewer: I now assign weights to the paths. Please tell me how to find the shortest route from A to C using Dijkstra's algorithm.

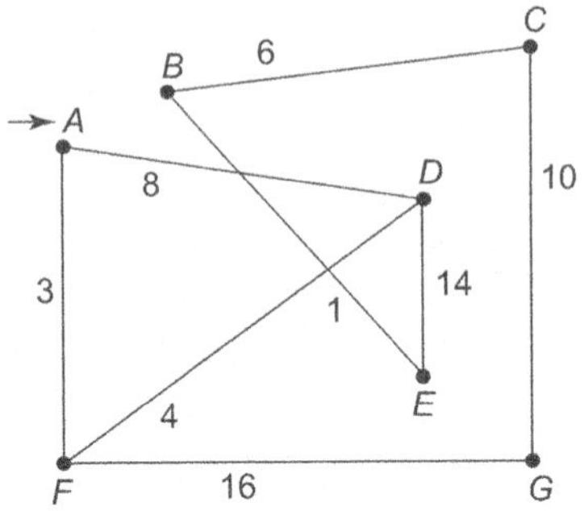

Sourav: Sir, for that, the algorithm to be used is as follows:

1. Mark all nodes as unvisited and their distances from A as ∞.
2. Select the current node (starting node A for first iteration) and find distances to its unvisited neighbors. AF = 3, AD = 8. Replace any higher values by smaller values.
3. Mark node A as visited node. It would not be revisited.
4. Go to the neighbor with the smallest distance and mark it as the current node (F in the first iteration).
5. Repeat steps 2 to 4 until all the nodes are visited.

In second iteration, distance to D is marked as 7.

Node D becomes the current node for third iteration.

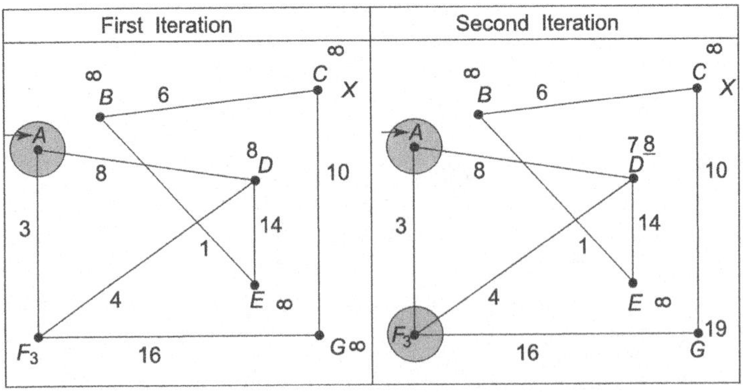

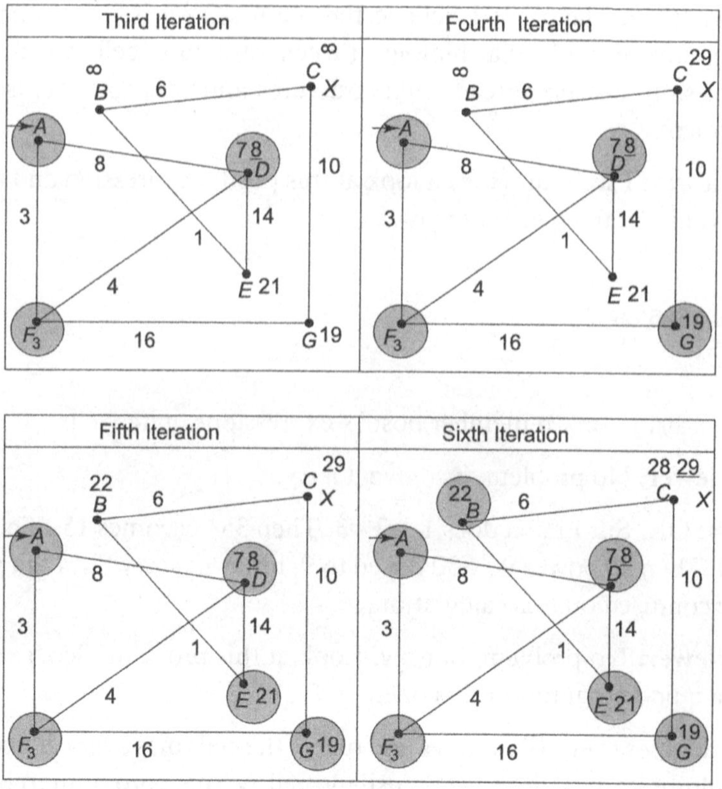

Node G becomes the current node for fourth iteration. Fifth iteration considers E as the current node and sixth iteration considers node B as the current node. The final iteration is done at node C and its calculated distance is set as 28.

The algorithm completes after seventh iteration as all the nodes have been marked visited.

Interviewer: That was a neat explanation. I must say it is a really good practice to walk through an algorithm on a piece of paper like this. Can you list any application of this algorithm?

Sourav: One of the common applications is for network communication. It is used for quick routing of the network traffic between the source and target systems. For example, when I try to download a video from a remote server, the data is sent over the shortest available path.

Interviewer: Your college is making you learn a lot of computers, especially data structures. Is that to prepare students for IT placements?

Sourav: It does help but I believe the main reason is the applications of computers in molecular biology. Protein structure, cell model, signal transmission, disease spread, etc.: structures and concepts are used just everywhere.

Interviewer: I see that. Have a look at this postfix expression and tell me what would be the resultant value:

```
12+5*2$9/52*-
```

Sourav: Sir, I don't remember postfix expressions quite well.

Interviewer: No problem, just give it a try.

Sourav: OK, Sir. First it does 1 + 2 =3. Then 35* becomes 15. Then 15 * 2 = 30. Then 30 power 9 ... 30 raised to 9, hmm ... sorry Sir, I am getting a little confused on this calculation.

Interviewer: No problem, Sourav. Look at this problem. See if you can write a quick program for this one.

A cell doubles every 10 minutes and one of the cells dies every 20 minutes. The culture starts at T = 0 with a single cell. Write a program to find the cell count at any given time in this culture.

Sourav: As cell doubles in 10 minutes, there should be 4 cells after 20 minutes but one dies, so there would be 3 cells after 20 minutes. Count will be 6 after 30 minutes and (12-1) = 11 after 40 minutes. That gives logic of 4n – 1. I can write a program to give count at durations that are multiples of 20. Shall I write it like that?

Interviewer: Go ahead.

Sourav: The count at any time would be one less than four times the count 20 minutes earlier. I have used recursive call to take care of this calculation. When it is the first 20 minutes, then the value would be 3. This condition will terminate the recursive calls.

```
/****************************************************************/
double count(int i)
{
        if (i == 1) return(3);
```

```
        else return((4 * count(i -1)) - 1);
}

/*************************************************************/

void main()
{
        int time;

        printf("\n Enter a time-duration that is a multiple of 20 : ");
        scanf("%d", &time);

        printf("Count of cells after %d minutes is : %lf", time, count(time/20));
}
/*************************************************************/
```

Interviewer: Why have you used double as return type for count() function?

Sourav: As the count would increase due to exponential growth, it might become an infinite loop with higher numbers being rotated back. Double would avoid this.

Interviewer: All right, Sourav, I have no more questions. Do you have any questions?

Sourav: Sir, may I look at that postfix problem once more?

Interviewer: By all means, if you really want to!

Sourav: Thanks, Sir.

12+5*2$9/52*-

First 1 + 2 =3. Then 3,5* becomes 15.

Then 15,2$ = 225, oh I had made a mistake here.

Then 225,9/ becomes 25

'25,5,2*-' it will be in reverse order = '25,10-' This becomes 15.

Sir, it will evaluate to 15.

Interviewer: Had you been thinking about it all the while?

Sourav: I could recollect the procedure to parse postfix expressions. So I thought of working on it once more.

Interviewer: Well done Sourav, I must say! And yes, thanks for helping me understand biotech a little bit.

Sourav: You are welcome, Sir. Have a good day, Sir!

SCENE 3

Pluto Computers' database gets one more record:

Name: Sourav

Final Decision – Select

Discipline Knowledge – Very Good

Computer Knowledge – Very Good

Aptitude – Very Good

Attitude – Very Good

Communication – Very Good

Additional comments: The candidate is very good at data structures despite being from a non-CS background, he can simplify difficult situations by easily drawing analogy between unrelated areas, and his thought process is quite logical as well.

SCENE 4

The interviewer happens to be an alumnus of the institute and the placement committee members request him for interview tips at the end of the day. He is too delighted to do this bit for his alma mater and decides to quote Sourav's performance to put his point forward.

"We generally look for students with the right attitude and aptitude. I will tell you how your friend Sourav fared so you can understand what I mean by that. He is from BioTech and I have very less idea of this field. Interviewing him would be a challenge for me if he does not know anything at all from computers. I might reject him saying he does not have the right attitude, otherwise he would have learnt at least something pertaining to the IT field before appearing for an IT company interview.

Else, I get an idea of his favorite subjects by talking to him, quickly pull up some questions on related topics from Google, and throw them at him. If he can make me understand the answers for them, mind you, if he gives correct answers and does not try to take undue advantage of my ignorance of the subject, I will be assured that he is good at his subjects and communication. I will also console myself saying that he can learn computers as he could learn his subjects. But the point remains is that his selection will still depend on his luck to be interviewed by someone who is willing to put in that sort of effort.

On the other hand, Sourav is good at his subjects and good at communication and answered all questions from his subjects quite well! In addition to that, he is very good at computers and made sure that I ask him questions from this field also by saying computer-related stuff in his introduction and by giving biotech questions' answers in computers' language. I could see that he has not merely studied, but understood the concepts also, as he could solve the given problems easily. I have seen computer students getting nervous on data structures while he was so confident and that gives him brownie points. This also shows that he is very good at aptitude, else he could not have analyzed the given problem and written a neat algorithm or program for that in the heat of an interview.

Summarily, if you are good at only computers or your discipline, your selection chances would follow a probabilistic curve dependent on the interviewer's mood. If you are good at both, then given the right attitude, you would be a sure-shot select. There is a third situation also, but, by now, you already know what is going to happen in that case!

❋ ❋ ❋

12

Civil's Soumya and Braino-Toniks

SCENE 1

It is the first time BT is letting Civil students appear and Soumya is clueless about what they could ask. She could not get through the two interviews she had appeared for earlier. The first interview focused on databases and she had no idea about them, and in the second one, the interviewer was a civil engineer by education and she could not justify reasons for the domain change after having displayed a good knowledge of civil engineering. Though she is upset about the fact, yet her confidence is not shaken. She has fully made up her mind to request the interviewer to ask her about C language only as that is all she knows from the computers' world. Fluid mechanics and surveying have already dropped out of her favorite subjects' list for IT companies. She has also edited out the surveying contest win mention from her latest resume.

SCENE 2

Interviewer: Hi Soumya, how are you?

Soumya: Good evening, Sir, I am fine, thank you. How are you?

Interviewer: I became all fine after reaching this beautiful town. You guys are lucky to be studying at such a lovely place.

Soumya: Yes, Sir, it is a lovely place, we go for frequent long walks around the hills. Did you go around the town?

Interviewer: Yea, we enjoyed the cable car ride and had a memorable walk down the *haat*.

Soumya: Did you get a chance to get a view from the bridge?

Interviewer: No, not yet, it is bit far I think. Is it worth going?

Soumya: Absolutely Sir! It gives a stupendous view of the valley and the hills.

Interviewer: Thanks for letting me know this. Our driver was not enthusiastic, but now we will convince him for going over there. Coming back to our discussion, have a look at this program and tell me what will happen if I try to compile or run it.

```
/*************************************************************/
void main()
{
    int a = 256, *p;
    float x = 256.0;
    p = &x;
    printf("\n Value at pointer p is : %d\n",*p);
}
/*************************************************************/
```

(Soumya: Thank God, Sir has started with C; please make him forget everything else about computers while he is talking to me.)

```
/*************************************************************/
```

Soumya: Sir, pointer p can refer to a 2-byte memory location. Float is 4 bytes. So p can point to the first 2 bytes, that is, partial number, and that too, the lower-order 2 bytes of the 4-byte float. So it will display the lower-order 2 bytes of 256 as a new integer.

Interviewer: How about this one?

```
/*************************************************************/
int main()
{
```

```
    static main;

    printf("\n main() is : ",main());
}
/**************************************************************/
```

Soumya: This program ... something is definitely wrong here: I think either it won't compile or run infinitely, one of these will happen ...

Interviewer: Hmm ... see this one ...

```
/**************************************************************/
void main()
{
    int val;
printf("\n Return values :  %d, %d, %d", val, scanf("%d", &val), printf("\nEnter Number\n"));
}
/**************************************************************/
```

Soumya: Let me see if printf() will work fine. Evaluating from the rightmost argument, it will print "Enter Number." Then scanf() will wait for the input value. This value gets assigned to val.

Yes, Sir, it will compile fine and print

val, 1, 14

where val is the entered value.

Interviewer: How did you get this 1 and 14?

Soumya: Scanf() stores the input value at the specified address and returns the number of arguments stored this way. In this case, we have a single argument and I am assuming it is entered correctly. Printf() returns the total number of characters printed by the control string. It is 14 characters in this case.

Interviewer: What will be printed by this statement?

```
/**************************************************************/
    static int val;
```

```
    printf("\n%d %d %d %d\n",++val,val++,++val,val++);
/*************************************************************/
```

Soumya: Out of the four arguments, ++val, val++, ++val, and val++, the rightmost val++ results in 1, then ++val makes it 2, then 3, and finally 4. So it will print

```
4 2 2 0
```

Interviewer: And what will happen for this program?

```
/*************************************************************/
void main()
{
    char x[9] = {'A', 'B', 'C', 'D', 'E'};
    char y[3] = {'F', 'G', 'H'};

    printf("\n %u \n",*&x[3]-*x++);
    printf("\n %s ",strcat(x,y));

}
/*************************************************************/
```

Soumya: It won't compile as array pointer x cannot be incremented like this.

Interviewer: If we comment out the first printf() statement?

Soumya: The string Y will be concatenated to string X. But there is no string termination character in Y. It should give some type of run-time error for missing character.

Interviewer: You mean to say it will compile successfully. Are you sure of that?

Soumya: Yes, Sir; C does not check arrays at compile time, so there would be no error thrown during compilation.

Interviewer: What will happen if the first printf() statement is modified as follows:

```
/***********************************************************/
{
    char x[9] = {'A', 'B', 'C', 'D', 'E'}, *p;
    p = x;
    printf("\n %u \n",*&x[3]-*++p);
}
/***********************************************************/
```

Soumya: Sir, *&x[3] is essentially equivalent to x[3] = D. "*++p" gives the value of address p + 1 = B. Difference between D and B would be 2.

Interviewer: Do you have any experience with linked lists?

Soumya: Yes, Sir.

Interviewer: Can you write a program to create a linked list with four elements?

Soumya: Yes, Sir. It can be written like this:

```
/***********************************************************/
//STRUCTURE DEFINITION FOR THE LINKED LIST NODES
struct list
{
    int no;
    struct list *next; //Pointer to point to a struct list type
};
/***********************************************************/
void main()
{
    int i=0;
    struct list *ptr;
/***********************************************************/
//FIRST NODE CREATION
    //Allot Four Byte memory for first node and assign first byte address to ptr
ptr= (struct list *)malloc(sizeof(struct list));
```

```
        ptr->no = i;
ptr->next=NULL;
        printf("\n New : %u %d \n",ptr,ptr->no);

/***********************************************************/
//MORE NODES ADDITION
        for(i=1;i<4;i++)
        {
                ptr->next = (struct list *)malloc(sizeof(struct list));
                ptr = ptr->next;
                ptr->no = i;
                printf("\n %u %d \n",ptr,ptr->no);
                ptr->next=NULL;
        }
}
/***********************************************************/
```

Interviewer: What is happening at this statement?

```
ptr= (struct list *)malloc(sizeof(struct list));
```

Soumya: I have used the malloc function and most part of this statement is the malloc syntax. The malloc function allocates n bytes at run time. The sizeof() operator is used to find this n depending on the type of structure being used. (struct list *) tells that the pointer returned for these bytes should be of type struct list.

Interviewer: Fine, which is better: an array or a list?

Soumya: Sir, for most of the applications, a list is better as it allows for dynamic sizes and easy insertion and deletion of elements. Also, if a node has to store multiple values, like four subject marks for a student, then it is very easy to define this in the form of a structure.

Interviewer: Very good, Soumya. What are your favorite subjects from civil engineering?

Soumya: Sir, my favorite subjects are engineering geology and transportation engineering.

Interviewer: What exactly in transportation engineering?

Soumya: You can ask anything.

Interviewer: Not like that, tell me some topics that you like.

Soumya: No, Sir, I won't say anything like that, I will get caught; you can ask me whatever you want to ask.

(Interviewer: This is not done Soumya; if I had to ask like that, I could have asked you questions on SOM and SDD directly. Do you really want me to do that?)

Interviewer: Let me see then: have you studied about highways, airports, tunnels and track design?

Soumya: Yes, Sir.

Interviewer: Have you also studied about GPS, GIS, etc.?

Soumya: Not yet, Sir; we will be studying about that in the final sem.

(Interviewer: As you are not ready to talk, I can be really mean with you and ask for Howrah Bridge truss analysis. But I won't do that as you have been good at C. Let me scratch my brains to recollect everything related to transportation and geology I have seen around and ask you questions on all of that!)

Interviewer: All right then! We see metro rail construction going around in all major cities now. Tell me everything about the tunneling technology being used there.

Soumya: Sir, we haven't studied urban tunneling like that but I have seen a Discovery Channel presentation on Delhi Metro. I know that a tunnel boring machine augmented with controlled rock blasting is being used for this purpose. TBM is a complex assembly by itself with a rotating steel head for cutting through the soil and a trailing system for muck removal, soil strengthening, and laying precast concrete segments. At places like Delhi and Jaipur, an earth pressure balance type of machine was used. It maintains the pressure balance constant, so that the buildings above do not feel any vibrations or undergo damage.

Interviewer: I had read that rails are of some special alloy and it is not possible to normally cut tracks. What is the special alloy used for rails?

Soumya: A lot of research is going on rail alloy combination. As far as I know, the rail strength and hardness is attributed to the high carbon content in steel. Manganese and molybdenum are also used for hardening.

Interviewer: I have seen markings on a couple of stretches on a highway, "Ecophalt Test Track." What is this ecophalt?

Soumya: Ecophalt is plastic mixed asphalt and it is more porous. It is supposed to be long-lasting as water would not stay on the road surface, but will be absorbed and drained via ducts. This will help avoid potholes and reduce repair costs.

Interviewer: In that case, what is the significance of "eco" in ecophalt?

Soumya: It is supposed to be eco-friendly. As it is porous in nature, it can be used for recharging underground water. It also puts waste plastic to a good use.

Interviewer: Reflective road markings are a boon to night driving. What makes these markings reflective?

Soumya: The markings are painted with micro glass beads while still wet. The glass beads are embedded in paint on drying. These glass beads exhibit retro-reflectivity, that is incident light is refracted back to the original direction. Thus, it is pure physics at play.

Interviewer: That's interesting! Tell me about four or five main areas that would have been considered for designing the new Hyderabad and Bangalore airports?

Soumya: Sir, I am not sure about these airports' design but I think the general considerations for airport design would have been followed.

Interviewer: General considerations like?

Soumya: Like site selection, overall size as per traffic forecast, runway and taxiway design, communication system, terminal design and location with respect to the runway, lighting and energy conservation, access from the city center, disaster management, etc.

Interviewer: That reminds me of the Fukushima earthquake. Tell me what is so special about Japanese buildings that allows them to withstand massive quakes while we saw Haiti was devastated?

Soumya: It is because of an earthquake-resistant building design.

Interviewer: What is special about such a design?

Soumya: The very first level is making the building stronger through steel reinforcement. Base isolation and vibration dampers are also used. In base isolation, the building is supported on flexible pads or rollers. This reduces the displacement forces impact on the building. In addition to this, dampers and other energy dissipation devices are also used there to absorb the quake impact.

Interviewer: Is there a way to test such a building design for performance before actual construction?

Soumya: Sir, it can be tested with the help of shake tables in labs. We can simulate earthquake shaking on such tables and see the impact of building prototypes standing on the table when its computer-controlled shaking is induced. Shake tables can have degrees of freedom from 1 to 6.

(Soumya: Am I talking a lot about civil again ... I think no, these questions pertain more to awareness about recent things. Anyways, let me be rejected for knowing more civil than for appearing stupid by not answering such questions.)

Interviewer: What is a degree of freedom and what are the six different degrees?

Soumya: Degree of freedom means the number of directions in which displacement and rotation are possible. Displacement is possible along all the three axes, that is, up and down, left and right, and forward and backward. Tilting left and right, forward and backward, and rotating or turning are the three degrees of rotational freedom.

Interviewer: Have you seen one?

Soumya: Yes, Sir, there is one in our institute but it has only two degrees of freedom.

Interviewer: There is a lot of awareness being spread about earthquake preparedness and seismic zones in India? What are these zones and what does the classification signify?

Soumya: As per the latest seismic map, there are four seismic zones in India: zones II, III, IV, and V. As per the Modified Mercalli Intensity (MMI) scale, these zones correspond to scales VI, VII, VIII, and IX, that is, from strong to violent earthquake impact zones. General building rules for any location depend on the seismic zone the location falls under. But for special structures like nuclear plants, etc., a specific seismic study of the area is additionally carried out.

(Interviewer: Hmm, so you do have an understanding of your favorite subjects; I can go on like this but there has to be a stop somewhere, so let it be here. Asking you civil questions was such a rigorous mind exercise for me.)

Interviewer: How would you handle a conflict in team: suppose you want to do something in one way and your teammate wants to do it in an entirely different style?

Soumya: I will discuss all the styles with the team along with the positive and negative sides. Then we can go for the best approach and sometimes even make the chosen approach better by incorporating some ideas from the other approaches.

Interviewer: How can you be so sure of handling it like this: do you have any experience?

Soumya: Yes, Sir, I faced a somewhat similar situation. Three of us were participating in a treasure hunt competition in the Tech Fest, and all three of us interpreted the clues very differently and felt that our individual interpretation was right. It was a sure-shot formula for losing. But I could mediate it like this and because our approach was very logical, we finally won.

Interviewer: They were friends but it might not work out in an office environment where people don't want to listen to you.

Soumya: In that situation, we will need to involve the manager in the discussion to arrive at a decision.

Interviewer: If you are sure that your viewpoint is the best one, would you not want to speak to the manager directly and try to convince him that your approach is the best way to go?

Soumya: I think we should not do that; involving everyone should be the right way.

Interviewer: Well said, Soumya! That was the last question I had to ask you today. Let me know if you have got any questions for me.

Soumya: Yes, Sir, can you please tell me about some computer-related areas that I should prepare for before joining?

Interviewer: That's a very good question, Soumya. It would become easy for you if you could get a basic understanding of Java and databases. I presume you are not familiar with these technologies as they are not mentioned in your CV!

Soumya: Yes, Sir, I am not familiar with them but I will start learning now.

Interviewer: Bye, Soumya.

Soumya: Thanks, Sir. Bye.

SCENE 3

Soumya still cannot digest that someone from a non-civil background could ask her so many questions about her so-called favorite subjects. She realizes that her discipline can be seen at work by people so directly. Though she is optimistic about the interview outcome, yet the second half of the discussion that focused on her discipline is making her doubtful.

While she is lost in these thoughts, the interviewer who had long back decided on her selection evaluates her performance objectively.

Discipline Knowledge – Good

Computer Knowledge – Very Good at C.

Communication – Very Good

Other Comments – Team player with leadership qualities.

SCENE 4

A junior colleague who had evaluated Soumya's group's GD performance remarks that she was the best among her group and asks about her interview performance. He is told that her name is on the list of final selects. He also wants to get more insight on her interview to help him understand how to handle civil background students. The interviewer summarizes the discussion for him.

Soumya had mentioned about good knowledge of C in her CV and that gave me a good starting point. I gave her few problems on that and realized that her knowledge is in sync with her CV. Then I gave her a couple of more problems to get an idea of her knowledge expanse. I was delighted to see that she understands operator precedence and associativity, pointers, arrays, strings, structures, lists, and dynamic memory allocation. That was enough for me to decide on her selection.

To do better justice to our evaluation form, I asked her about her favorite subjects and she mentioned geology and transportation. I wanted the discussion to go very open-ended from there onward as I was wary of framing questions from such fields. I wanted her to talk about the things she found interesting but she turned out to be quite stubborn and refused to talk like that. She wanted me to pose questions: now that could have been a challenging situation for me if the mentioned subjects were not generic. That could have spelled disaster for her as well. As I was already biased toward selecting her, I gave her a second chance by straining my brain for questions on highways, airports, tracks, earthquakes, etc. As you know I have worked on GIS, so wanted to ask questions on it also but that is yet to be studied by them.

Her replies to these questions did not disappoint me though. She knows concepts and is quite aware of recent developments. Finally, I had to check her compatibility for team work as she had demonstrated quite a stubborn attitude earlier. Her overall performance followed a sine-wave cycle with a crest, trough, and then a crest again, and that second crest helped her sail through.

* * *

13

Electronics' Aarav Excels at CVM Inc.

SCENE 1

Aarav is one of the few students who could clear the written test and the GD round. Given the very low percentage of selections till now, there is a general apprehension in the minds of all the students waiting for the interview round. This is further increased by the fact shared during PPT that the interviewer is an embedded systems expert. Aarav has brought a fat file along with him for his innumerable certificates and is silently praying for the interviewer to be impressed by them. He is silently rehearsing his introduction and going through probable questions. Very soon he is called for the interview.

SCENE 2

Aarav: Hello Sir, this is Aarav.

Interviewer: Hi Aarav, take a seat please.

Aarav: Thanks, Sir.

Interviewer: How did you find the test?

Aarav (*smiling*): It was easy.

Interviewer (*happily*): Good to hear that someone found it easy; many of your friends were complaining that it was quite tough. Tell me more about your final-year project.

Aarav: Sir, we have developed a low-cost, lightweight, and robust system to detect LPG leakage. It consumed low power and was found very reliable when we tested it in our hostel kitchen.

Interviewer: How does it detect LPG?

Aarav: We have used Figaro LPG sensor TGS 6810 for this purpose in the circuit.

Interviewer: Tell me more about this circuit.

Aarav (*enthusiastic*): Sir, we have used a bell alarm system and this is being fed from the Figaro sensor circuit. As per the datasheet, this sensor can detect low concentrations of butane and propane and generate an output voltage in direct ratio of the gas concentration. We finalized the TGS 6810 model because it generated approximately 8 mV signal at detectable but still safe gas concentration levels. This signal was amplified through the transistor circuit and drove the alarm system.

The block diagram for this project is like this:

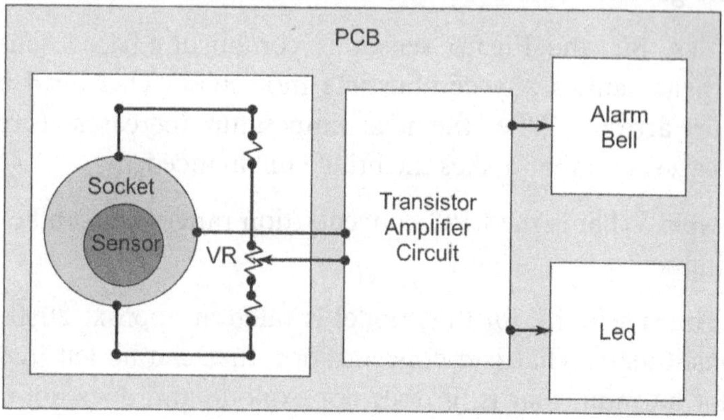

Setting the variable resistor VR was the most difficult task and we had to take continuous output readings for 3 days in open ground. This was needed to remove any false alarms. Then we had to check if the circuit was still able to detect LPG presence.

(At this point, Aarav hands out a printout to the interviewer)

This is the paper that we wrote after completing this test. We have recorded all the measurements and circuit behavior at various resistance values. We did some additional analysis to supplement this data that can serve as a guideline for others.

Interviewer (*curious*): Why is this VR so important?

Aarav: Sir, for normal conditions, the circuit works like a balanced bridge. This VR is used for bridge balancing under a given air condition and temperature.

Interviewer: How did you create the PCB?

Aarav: We did the field testing on breadboard only and decided on all the component parameters. We used ExpressPCB for PCB layout.

Interviewer: Did you manufacture the PCB yourself or was it outsourced?

Aarav: Sir, we got it done from outside. We had created the first one but that did not work properly and all the components including the sensor were wasted. But, it was us who designed the original working circuit on breadboard. We did not take any external help in that.

Interviewer (*probing further*): Do you have any idea how this sensor detects the gas molecules?

Aarav: Yes, Sir; the Figaro sensor is combustion-based sensor. The detector head ignites any combustible molecules. This head is placed inside a fire arrester. When the head temperature increases, its resistance also increases, and that makes the bridge unbalanced.

Interviewer: What is the LPG concentration range that can be detected in this manner?

Aarav: The sensitivity for this model is rated at approx. 2000 ppm for LPG constituents. That is a concentration that can be felt by us but it is still not harmful; that is, it does not explode and does not choke on inhaling.

(Aarav again refers to the printout lying on the table)

We have also included this section 4 for the factors to be considered while selecting a sensor type. These values are also mentioned in this section.

Interviewer: Have you heard about the 3D transistor technology recently announced by Intel?

Aarav (*excitedly*): Yes, Sir; there was almost euphoria in the Electronics Department the day this news came. Intel has converted the planar gate in the MOSFET to a three-dimensional structure, thereby increasing the inversion channel length and achieving fully depleted operation. I will draw the figure of both the planar and 3D transistors as per the Intel's official document to highlight the differences between the two.

The gate oxide is shown in black and the inversion layer is shown in white. As the transistor size decreases, the inversion layer gets shortened and it cannot be shortened beyond a maximum limit. In 3D transistor, the silicon substrate has been made to protrude upward above the drain and source surface in the third direction, thereby increasing the length of the inversion layer. This has been called the fin and the gate oxide surrounds it on all three exposed sides. That's how it has got the name tri-gate also.

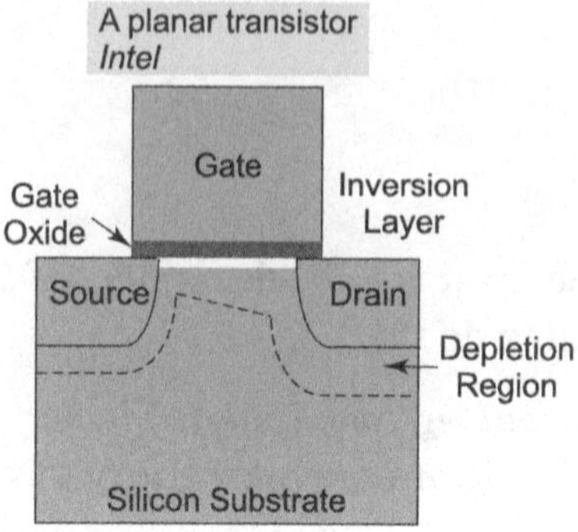

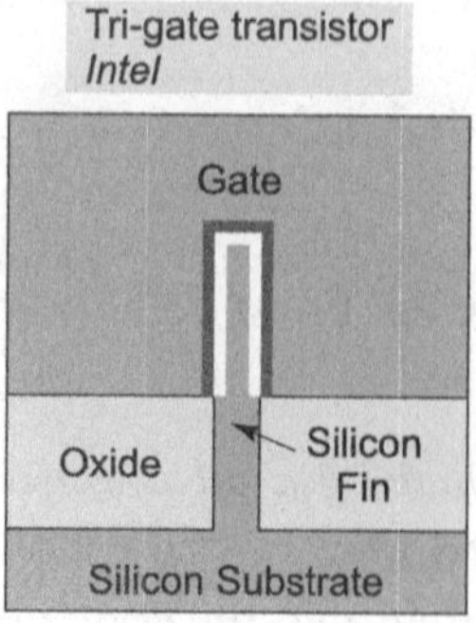

Interviewer: That was from a latest development in the field. Let's go back to the beginning of the semiconductor era. Have a look at this very simple circuit and tell me what it might be doing.

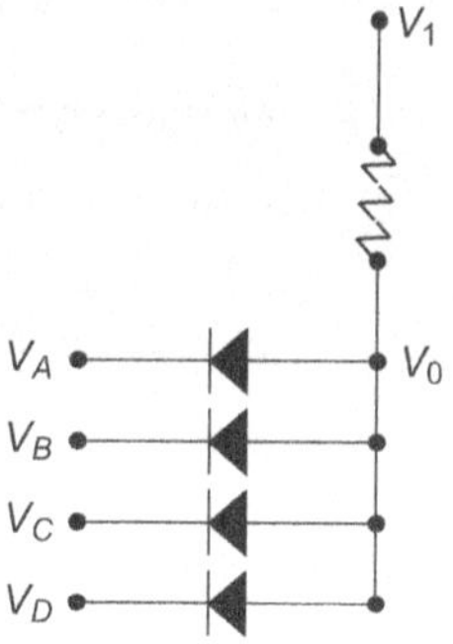

$V_1 = V_A = V_B = V_C = V_D$

Aarav: Sir, V_O will be equal to V_I as none of the diodes are conducting right now. This circuit can be generalized as a four-input AND circuit, where V_O would be high when all of the inputs are high. If any of the inputs will be low, that diode will start conducting, hence V_I would be dropped across the resistor and V_O would become zero.

$$V_O = V_A . V_B . V_C . V_D$$

Interviewer: If I have to twist it to make it work as an OR circuit, how can I do that?

Aarav: That can be accomplished reversing the diodes' directions and then by removing V_I and grounding this terminal.

$$V_O = V_A + V_B + V_C + V_D$$

Interviewer: For a BJT, the value for α is to be determined if β is given and vice versa. Write a C program to do this.

Aarav (*looking a bit confused but talking confidently*): Sir, for BJT $\beta = \alpha / 1 - \alpha$ and $\alpha = \beta / \beta + 1$. The C program can make use of this formula. I will write down the code now.

(Aarav: But how will the program accept the characters α and β? I think I will need to accept the ASCII values for these characters … Idea! There is no need for the exact symbols as the program won't know the difference between "α" and "α.")

```
/*************************************************************/
void main()
{
        char input;
        float val;
        printf("\n Enter a for alpha, b for beta \n");
        scanf("%c",&input);
/*************************************************************/
        switch (input)
        {
                case 'a' :
```

```
        case 'A' :
            printf("\n Enter alpha value now \n");
            scanf("%f",&val);
            printf("\n For alpha : %f, beta = %f \n", val, val / (1 - val));
            break;

/*************************************************************/

        case 'b' :
        case 'B' :
            printf("\n Enter beta value now \n");
            scanf("%f",&val);
            printf("\n For beta : %f, alpha = %f \n", val, val / (1 + val));
            break;

/*************************************************************/

        default :
            printf("\n Entered an incorrect identifier \n");
    }
}

/*************************************************************/
```

(The interviewer is keenly observing Aarav develop the program. He comments to himself, "Good to see he has made it case insensitive and included the default case as well.")

Interviewer: What will happen if I enter 1 for alpha or -1 for beta?

Aarav: Sorry Sir, it won't work then. It will give run-time error for division by zero in that case.

Interviewer: And what if I enter negative values for alpha or beta?

Aarav: That would distort the results. This can be avoided by including if conditions to check for range. Shall I include the conditions now?

Interviewer: That's fine; no need. Does C support some inbuilt mechanism for range checking?

Aarav (*baffled*): I am not sure, Sir. I have never come across any such function.

Interviewer: Are TV and RADAR included as subjects in your curriculum?

Aarav: Yes, Sir, they are.

Interviewer: And I am sure you must have heard about the Seals helicopter that was left behind at Abbottabad, haven't you?

Aarav: Yes, Sir, I know about that.

Interviewer: In that case I assume you must have also heard about its alleged stealth design to avoid RADAR detection. You have to explain how stealth technology works in general; that is, how is it possible to avoid RADAR detection?

Aarav: Sorry, Sir, I don't know how it works. May I take a guess at that?

Interviewer: Why not, please go ahead!

Aarav (*thinking deeply*): RADAR detects an object when the RADAR waves hit the body and are reflected back. If there is no back-reflection, the RADAR believes that the area is clear. So to avoid detection, the object will have to do something so that the waves hitting it are not reflected back to the RADAR. For that the body surface structure might be designed to reflect the waves in other directions and to cancel a near-180-degree reflection. Another possibility might be that the object absorbs the waves completely like a black hole. I think it might be one of these two or a combination of both that is being used for stealth technology.

Interviewer (*impressed*): Hmm ... that was quite an intelligent guess! Like restaurant menu options for cheese-based curry, the market is flooded with different types of TVs nowadays: LCD, Plasma, Digital, HD, etc. What are all these types?

Aarav: Sir, the basic TV used was the CRT or the cathode ray tube based. It was an analog TV. It is bulky, as the distance between the electron gun and screen has to be maintained. Digital TVs use one or other type of digital technology. LCD technology is one such type.

Liquid crystals are substances which that their transparency on application of voltage. A combination of three such LCDs along with three color filters forms a pixel. Also, the level of transparency change is subject to the applied voltage. There are generally 256 levels supported by present-day LCDs. A matrix arrangement of such pixel units and an activation system to charge pixels forms the LCD TV. It can be made very thin, and unlike CRTs, their thickness won't need to increase for supporting a larger screen. Also, they would be free of gravity- or magnetic field-based distortions of the electron stream, as happens in a CRT.

A plasma TV is very similar to an LCD TV in its screen design. The only difference is that in a plasma TV, the pixel unit is made up of fluorescent lights instead of LCDs. The light-producing element in such lights is an ionized gas mix or plasma.

HD means high definition. Two aspects determine the level of definition as standard, enhanced, or high. For HD, the aspect ratio is 16:9. Normal CRTs have an aspect ratio of 4:3. As we can see, it gives a wider screen and a more realistic view of the screen. Next is the resolution or the number of pixels. HDTV calls for a screen resolution of 1920 × 1080 ...

Interviewer: That would be sufficient. I see reading novels is your hobby; who are your favorites?

Aarav: I like the works of Chetan Bhagat, Dan Brown, Jeff Archer, and Oscar Wilde.

Interviewer: That's quite a variety, isn't it?

Aarav: Yes, Sir; their writing is very different from each other and that keeps me refreshed.

Interviewer: Can I expect a sermon on cryptography from a Dan Brown fan?

Aarav: I am sorry, Sir; I did not get that.

Interviewer: I mean can you tell me something about cryptography? Let me be more specific: can you tell me about the RSA algorithm?

Aarav (*delighted on being asked an expected question*): Yes Sir. RSA is one of the earliest known and best used public key algorithms. A receiver system generates a pair of public and private keys. It shares the public key with the sender system willing to communicate with it. The sender system encrypts the message with the public key thus received and sends the encrypted message. This message can be decrypted only by using the receiver's private key. Any other intruder on the system won't be able to decrypt this message within any reasonable time frame.

Interviewer: Can you write down the algorithm and give an example implementation in C?

Aarav: Yes, Sir. The algorithm is as follows:

1. Select two big prime numbers, p and q.
2. Calculate n = p * q.
3. Calculate z = (p-1) * (q-1).
4. Select a number d that is relatively prime to z, that is GCD(d,z) = 1. "d" is the private key.
5. Calculate e such that (e * d) % z = 1.
6. Share n and e with the sender system. These are called the public key.
7. To encrypt a plain text P to cipher text C, use the logic $C = P^e$ * (mod n).
8. To decrypt C to P, the only logic that can be used is $P = C^d$ * (mod n).

The strength of the algorithm comes from the fact that it needs the value of "d" to decrypt the message. For that, p and q need to be known. If the originally selected values of p and q were quite large, it is quite difficult to try to guess the prime factors of a much bigger n.

Now for the C implementation, I will write a program assuming that external functions isprime() and hcf() are already available. Also, I will be using very small values for all the variables for the sake of this program.

```
/*************************************************************/

//Section 1 - Library files

#include<stdio.h>

#include<stdlib.h> //For rand() function

#include<time.h> //For randomize() function as it uses a time-based seed

#include<math.h> //For pow() function

/*************************************************************/

//Section 2 – Variable Declaration

void main()

{

        int p,q,n,z,d,e,loop=0,plain,cipher; //Opted for int as values will be small
for demo
```

```
    printf("\n Enter plaintext number \n");
    scanf("%d", &plain);

/**************************************************************/

//Section 3 - Select prime number p

    while (loop == 0)
    {
        randomize(); //Reset the random number generator
        p = rand() % 10; //Get a random number < 10
        loop = isprime(p); //Check if it is prime
    }

/**************************************************************/

//Section 4 - Select prime number q

    loop = 0;
    while (loop == 0)
    {
        randomize();
        q = rand() % 10 + 10; //Get a number between 10 and 19 to avoid
p=q
        loop = isprime(q);
    }

/**************************************************************/

//Section 5 - Calculate n, z, d

    n = p * q;
    z = (p-1) * (q-1);
    loop = 0;
    while (loop != 1)
    {
        randomize();
        d = rand() % 10; //Get a small d
```

```
            loop = hcf(d,z);
        }

/************************************************************/

//Section 6 - Calculate e

        loop = 0;
        for (e=1; loop!=1;)
        {
            e++; //Get corresponding e
            loop = (e * d) % z;
        }

/************************************************************/

//Section 7 - Calculate ciphertext and plaintext

/*pow() returns a double value and modulus cannot be found for it*/
        cipher = (long unsigned int)pow(plain,e) % n;

        printf("\n plaintext number is : %d, ciphertext is :%d, plaintext again is : %lu
\n",plain, cipher,((long unsigned int)pow(cipher,d)%n));
}

/************************************************************/
```

(Now Aarav takes the interviewer through the entire program and marks comments at the places he is asked for explanation.)

Interviewer: I understand that, Aarav. Thanks for the patient explanation. Now comes the reward time. Congratulations, you would be receiving the CVM offer letter shortly!

Aarav (*visibly delighted*): Thank you, Sir, thank you very much.

SCENE 3

Aarav's friends break into instant celebration with the news of his selection. Being one of the two CVM selects, he is asked by everyone for his interview details. He almost blurts out that his certificate file was not even asked about. He confesses that he had never dreamed of writing a computer program for RSA encryption and decryption. Till now, he was under the impression that such concepts are for understanding purpose and not for any real implementation. At the same time he confides that the interview was a very good experience, which he will remember for a long time.

SCENE 4

In the meanwhile, the interviewer completes the mandatory analysis for the selected candidates.

Aarav has implemented his major project based on thorough analysis and knows the project in and out. He is good at C programming and is not someone who tries to learn programming by heart. This could be seen by the way he could write code for the unusual situations given.

He has a good knowledge of his discipline's subjects. He is also well aware of the recent advancements in the field like a true technologist.

His attitude is commendable. He is straight-talking, honest, and polite. At the same time, he is good at communication, is intelligent, and possesses a good engineering aptitude.

Based on the above analysis, he is recommended for a fresher position at CVM Inc.

14

Computers' Akrit Meets His Idol from Calculinks Inc.

SCENE 1

Akrit is looking forward to the interview. Worrying about the interview outcome is the last thing on his mind. He is simply ecstatic at the opportunity to meet his idol, the author of the IT Systems book who works at Calculinks. He owes his current knowledge of the field to the conceptual base provided by this book. Like few others from his class, he is finding it hard to wait for his turn. In the excitement, he does not even notice that he has forgotten his CV.

SCENE 2

Akrit (*vivacious*): Hello Sir, very good afternoon! I am Akrit from the Computer Science Department.

Interviewer: Good afternoon, Akrit. You seem to be very happy!

Akrit (*smiling*): Yes Sir, I am happy I got a chance to be interviewed by you. When I joined college, I had very poor knowledge about the computer field. Your book helped me understand all the concepts. That's why I am very happy to meet you.

Interviewer (*with renewed interest*): Oh really! I am glad you found it useful. Can I please see your resume?

Akrit: Yes, Sir.

(Akrit searches for the resume in his file and suddenly realizes his mistake. He feels dejected about creating such a bad first impression.)

Akrit (*regretting*): I am very sorry, Sir; it is misplaced somehow. Sorry, Sir ...

Interviewer (*passively*): In that case, a detailed introduction would do.

(Akrit hastily rewords his introduction to suffice for the missing CV)

Akrit: Sir, I am Akrit, final-year computer science student at the MIIT. I have got a 7.2 CGPA till sixth semester. I completed class XII from CBSE board with 82 percent marks. I am working on the library management system for my final-year project. I have participated in RIM Techfest and our team got the third prize there. My hobbies are painting and singing and I regularly participate in all cultural activities.

(Hidden from Akrit's view, the interviewer makes a note of all the points mentioned by him.)

Interviewer: What are your favorite subjects?

Akrit: Computer Networks and Operating Systems.

Interviewer: What is the technology used for your final-year project?

Akrit: Sir, it is VB front-end and SQL Server DBMS back-end.

Interviewer: You have no interest in either of these technologies or programming?

Akrit (*with a start*): No, Sir, not like that. I like these subjects also.

Interviewer: What is IPv4?

Akrit: It refers to Internet Protocol version 4. It is a communication protocol being extensively used for data transfer over the Internet. It is a network layer protocol and forms the backbone of the internet. It defines the structure of the data packet to be transmitted over the network.

Interviewer: What type of structure does it define?

Akrit: The packet structure includes a header and the data part. Inside the header, the first 20 bytes are mandatory. Apart from this there can be 40 bytes for optional fields. After the header, the data part starts. The limitation on the overall packet size is of 64 kilobytes.

I can draw the structure for it along with the main parts I remember as of now:

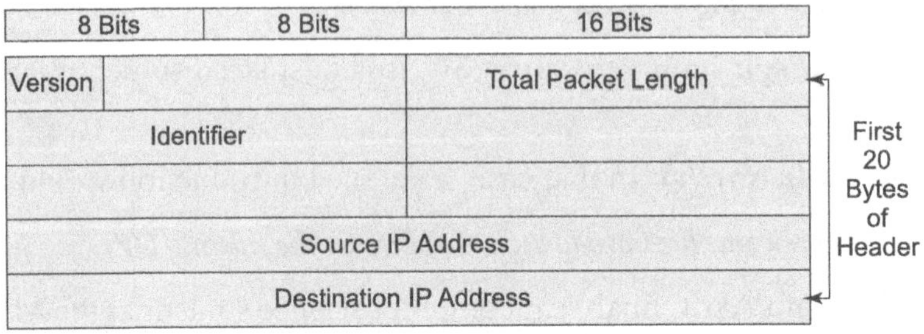

Here the 4-bit Version field specifies the protocol version. For example, v4, v6, etc.

Bytes 3 and 4 specify the total packet length. As 16 bits are being used, a max. size of 16K is possible.

The identifier field comes next. It helps in identifying the packets belonging to a common request. For example, I open two browser sessions and start downloading two movies. Then all the packets coming for one browser session, that is, the movie content, will have the same identifier.

Bytes 12–16 store the originating host IP address and bytes 17–20 store the target host IP address.

This structure clearly shows why IPv4 supports 32-bit addresses only, that is, an address of the format 192.168.1.1. Here each of these dot-separated numbers is used for denoting one byte.

Interviewer: How do these numbers 192 or 168 or 1 denote a byte?

Akrit: Sir, 192 in decimal is equivalent to 11000000 in binary. Similarly 1 would be equivalent to 00000001. In this manner, the maximum number might be 255 or FF or 11111111.

Interviewer: What is different in IPv6?

Akrit: The main features in IPv6 are a longer address support, 16 bytes to be precise, simplified header structure for faster packet processing by the router, and service quality, which is becoming important with multimedia channel increase.

Interviewer: Can you throw some more light on its header structure?

Akrit: Sure, Sir. The IPv6 compulsory header is 40 bytes long, mostly due to extra bytes allocation for address fields.

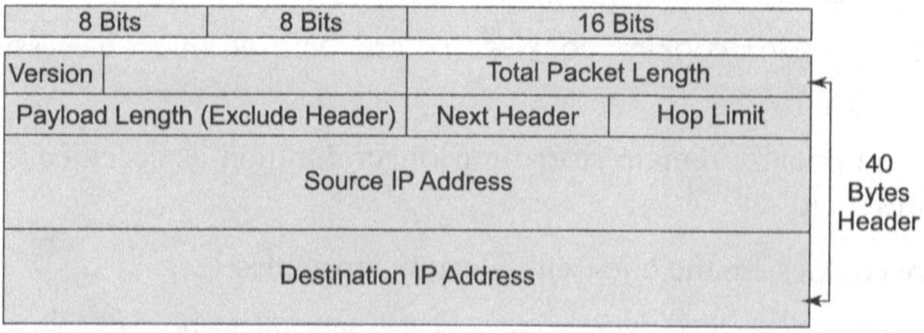

In this format, the Version is still the same.

The length is modified to denote the actual data or the payload length. That is, it does not count 40 header bytes.

Next Header is for specifying optional headers, if needed.

Hop Limit determines the maximum hops a packet can make before being declared a lost packet.

The address fields come next. The new address length is of 16 bytes.

Interviewer: And how are these address values written?

Akrit: The new notation is writing the addresses in hexadecimal format separated by colons. There can be maximum eight groups of four hex digits.

For example, 8000::192:FFEC:1234. Any "all zero" combinations in between can be skipped as in this case, there were four groups of '0000' in between '8000' and '192' and they have been skipped.

Interviewer: What are cookies and their various types?

Akrit: A cookie is essentially a file stored by a website on the client machine that was used to visit this website. On the initiation of a session, a cookie is generally sent by the site to the client side. When the client side creates a request to the same site in future, the previously stored cookie is also sent along with the request. A possible use of this feature is that the site builds a customized interface for the user based on his preferences.

A cookie has many parts. The domain name identifies the site which sent the cookie. Content stores the actual information, for example, user name or news preferences, etc. The 'Expires' field stores the duration for which the cookie will remain stored on the client hard disk. The 'Secure' field setting allows that cookie to be used for HTTPS sessions only.

There are session cookies: cookies that are removed once the session is over.

Persistent cookies remain stored for longer duration as specified by the 'Expires' field.

Secure cookies are the ones with 'Secure' attribute set.

Third-party cookies are the most controversial ones. The domain name for such cookies is not the actual visited site, but a third party which had placed an explicit or hidden link to its site on the visited site. Such cookies are used by advertisers to profile target customers and choke their inboxes with spam mails.

Interviewer: What are Bluetooth, Wi-Fi, and WLL? Do they refer to the same stuff or are they different?

Akrit: Sir, all three of these are IEEE standards for wireless communication, but for different purposes. Bluetooth is standard 802.15 and it is used for connecting peripherals to a master device. Cable-less keyboard and mouse communicating with CPU, or a hands-free device communicating with a cell phone are the examples. The signal range is quite small, up to a few meters. Also, these peripherals work in slave mode, that is, they cannot initiate or control communication. This also implies the slaves cannot talk to other slaves directly.

Wi-Fi or standard 802.11 is the next level. It is wireless LAN. We can use our laptops to connect to the Internet in our hostels using Wi-Fi just like we access the Internet using a LAN cable in the Computer Center. The range is a few hundred feet.

WLL, or the wireless local loop, is the standard 802.16. It runs over a few kilometers and is supposed to provide quick wireless connectivity between the ISP and the end user. For example, if instead of using cables we get directly connected with a telephone exchange, then it forms a WLL. The WLL operation frequency is much higher than the other two.

We can have a quick idea of this through the following diagram:

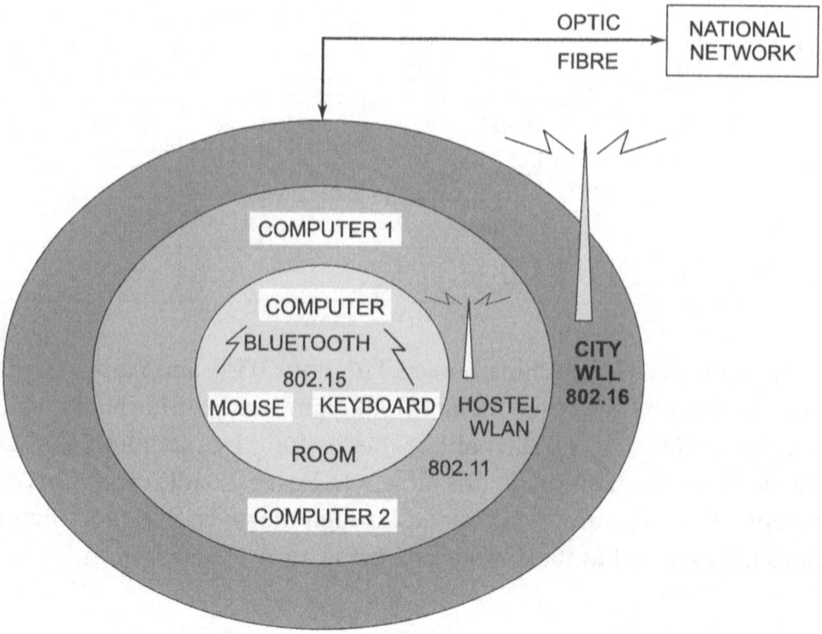

(Interviewer: He has prepared well for his favorite subject. Let me check if he can do any coding.)

Interviewer: This visual summary is good. Now, let's see what you are doing in your project.

Akrit: We are implementing a library management system. This will be used for issuing books to students and keeping track of the inventory. Right now, we have a token system. At the beginning of every semester, students are provided three token cards. These tokens need to be updated every semester and it creates a lot of work for the library department. All this would be avoided with this system. Also, a book reservation system would be possible and the student making reservation would be informed through email. We are yet to start work on the reservation module.

We are using SQL Server as the back-end database and Visual Basic as the front-end for this system. We have created tables like BOOK_DETAILS, STUDENT_DETAILS, and FINE_DETAILS.

The BOOK_DETAILS table has the following fields and sample data:

Book ID	Copy No	Book Name	Author Name	Issued Flag	Student Id	Date of Issue	Return Date
101	1	Let Us C	Yashwant Kanetkar	Y	4	1/4/2011	1/18/2011
101	2	Let Us C	Yashwant Kanetkar	Y	7	2/2/2011	2/16/2011
101	3	Let Us C	Yashwant Kanetkar				
102	1	The Complete Reference Java	Herbert Schildt	Y	3	1/21/2011	2/4/2011
102	2	The Complete Reference Java	Herbert Schildt	Y	15	2/7/2011	2/21/2011
103	1	Fundamentals of Computers	V Rajaraman				
104	1	Computer Networks	Andrew S Tanenbaum				
104	2	Computer Networks	Andrew S Tanenbaum				

The first form is for searching books. The Book Title and Author combo boxes are built by selecting distinct BookName and AuthorName values from the BOOK_DETAILS table. This is done by including a hidden data element which points to this table. On Form_Load() event, this data element's RecordSource is refreshed through the given SQL and then the values are assigned to the combo box using an AddItem option.

Interviewer: Can you write down that code?

Akrit: Yes, Sir.

```
/***********************************************************/
Private Sub Form_Load()
Dim Sqlstring As String

Sqlstring = "Select distinct BookName, AuthorName from BOOK_DETAILS"

With dataBookDtls
```

```
    .Recordsource = Sqlstring
    .Refresh

    Do until .Recordset.EOF
        cboBookTitle.AddItem .Recordset!BookName
        cboAuthor.AddItem .Recordset!AuthorName
        .Recordset.Movenext
    Loop
End With

/***********************************************************/
```

Interviewer: All right; what happens next?

Akrit: The user can make a selection and click on the "FetchBookDetails"; the Click Event code identifies the selection made and sets the global dimensions for Book Title and AuthorName with these values. Next it checks for the count of records from the BOOK_DETAILS table where the IssuedFlag is null. If the count is zero, it takes the smallest return date from the table. Then it activates the "Book Not Available" form, which looks like this:

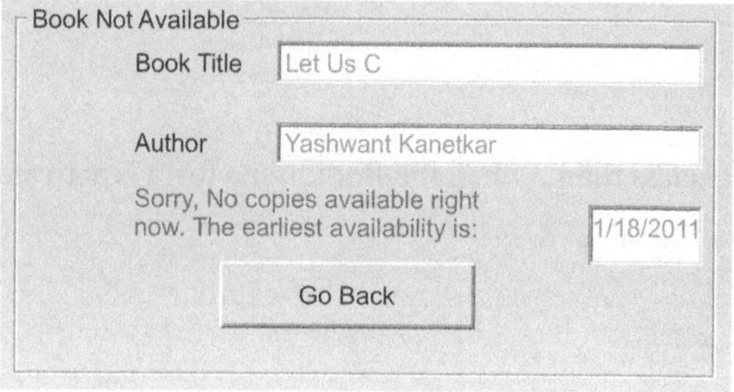

If the count is greater than zero, it fetches the record where the IssuedFlag is Null and CopyNo is smallest. Then the 'Enter Student ID' form is activated. This form shows all the fields except Student ID as disabled. The student id is entered and the "Fetch Student Details" button is clicked.

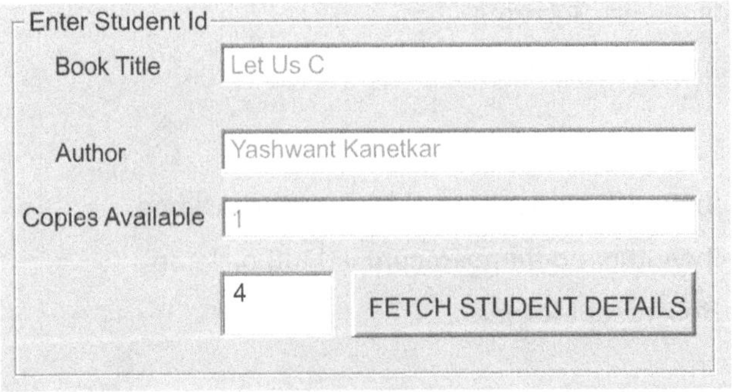

This click event counts the number of records in the BOOK_DETAILS table for the entered ID. If the count is 3, then the Student Name is fetched from the STUDENTS_DETAILS table and the "Student Not Eligible" form is activated. It tells that the student has been issued three books and cannot be issued any more books.

If the count is less than 3, then the Book Issue form is activated.

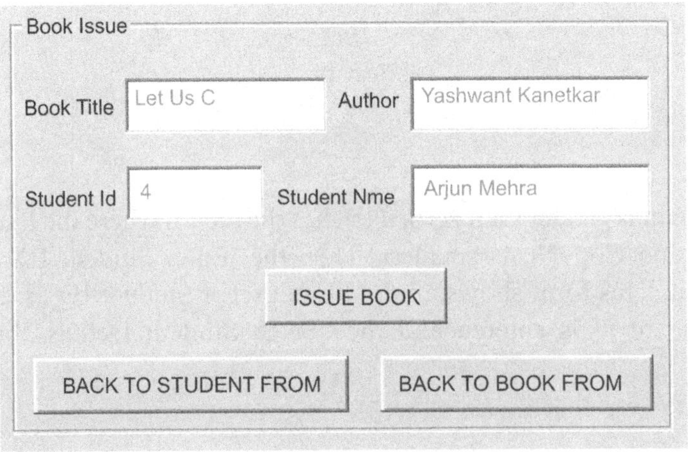

When the "Issue Book" button is clicked, the corresponding record in the BOOK_DETAILS table is updated. The studentID, issuedFlag, DateofIssue, and ReturnDate fields are assigned values. ReturnDate is an auto-calculated value. A success message is displayed and the "Issue Book" button disappears after that.

This completes the part of the project we have completed till now.

Interviewer: That's really elaborate and complete! It's not common to find student projects completed to this extent. And I liked the modular approach you are following. You have implemented a basic end-to-end functionality. Now you are going to expand it. It's pretty much like the way projects are implemented in IT!

Akrit: Thank you, Sir.

Interviewer: I want to hear about a few major challenges you faced in this project.

Akrit: Yes, Sir. It was very difficult getting started on this. We were not able to connect to the database. Then we tried using an Access database. That worked fine, but it had lot of problems, like we could not write queries. We had to read data from the STUDENT_DETAILS table that is already present with the administration department. So, using Access was forcing us to duplicate that table data.

Another problem faced was getting the BookTitle dropdown: we could scroll through the records one by one, but not display them all at one time, and then we learnt about "AddItem." We wanted to give flexibility for searching by partial text in this field. For that we needed to use wildcards in SQL. We knew about the concept, but had not used it before, so getting the SQL statement strings right through concatenation and wildcards was initially difficult.

Identifying the selected value was also a bit difficult. So we had to try that out for days.

Actually, we faced some problem or the other as soon as we added a new element. We had to work to solve that. We could not approach our guide many times as he has been busy arranging for a national conference.

(Interviewer: I am in a hurry today; let me wind up this one now. Anyways, poor Akrit needs a break; his throat must be dry by talking for so long!)

Interviewer: Your college must be proud of your team for doing this really useful work for them. All right then, Akrit, listening to your detailed explanation was a nice experience.

Akrit: Thank you, Sir.

(Akrit does not get the hint that the interview is over and stays behind expecting more questions.)

Interviewer: Yes, you waiting for something?

Akrit (*panicking*): No, Sir … Oh, is the interview over?

Interviewer (*smiling*): Yes.

Akrit (*calm again*): I am sorry; I could not understand that. I am very happy I got this opportunity to talk to you. Good day, Sir!

SCENE 3

Without even knowing about the result, Akrit is on cloud nine. Repeated attempts by his friends to make him feel foolish about forgetting the CV fail. They now suspect that he has managed to get a friend request on Facebook from the interviewer. In the meanwhile, the interviewer gives his comments on his performance.

Subject Knowledge – Good

Subjects Checked – Computer Networks, VB, Database

Project Description – Excellent

Overall Impression – Intelligent, organized, team player, visionary

Result – Selected

SCENE 4

As an attempt to kill time waiting for the dinner, the Calculinks team decides to share their most unique experiences of the day. Akrit's name immediately comes to his interviewer's mind and so he speaks about him.

"It was an easy interview for me. I didn't have to think of lot of questions for him, all I had to do was to probe a little further to get a confirmation that he understood the things he was talking about and was not a mere muggu. In fact, it was one of the rare occasions I spoke so less, and listened so much, during a student interview.

The technical discussion could start on a positive note as he had either mentioned a subject that was truly his favorite or had revised it quite well. He definitely has a good knowledge and the length at which he could speak on a topic reflects that. Otherwise students are generally wary of in-depth discussions as that has the potential to expose chinks in the façade of their artificial intelligence.

The best thing was his project. It is not that he had glanced through his project file for the sake of the interview. He has been actually working on it and trying to complete it in a logical manner. The reply to the last question truly authenticated that; otherwise, I hear students often mention software installation, deciding on the topic, guide and features to be included, getting guide's approval on those features, etc., as the real challenges. Following a step-by-step and modularized approach toward project completion clearly shows that he has a vision and is quite organized.

Coming to the soft skills, he is really gifted there! He realized that his CV was missing and got upset for a moment but regained his composure the very next moment. I could see that he had reworded his introduction to compensate for the missing CV. Such a composed and dynamic personality is good to have around."

15

Electronics' Inaas is Grilled by Coders International

SCENE 1

Inaas is quite happy about his written test performance. After all, the efforts put in to procure the paper from MIIT, the institute Coders International visited earlier, paid off. The majority of the questions at SUIT were repeat questions. Known well for his sharp tongue, he is quite confident of clearing the GD round. In the run-up for the campus preparation, he has attended many mock interviews and fared quite well there. Armed with such a combination of skill and preparation, he has already assumed his final selection.

SCENE 2

Interviewer: Tell me about yourself.

Inaas: Sir, this is Inaas. I am doing my final year of engineering in electronics from SUIT. About my family background, my parents are in government service. I have an elder sister who is doing MBBS. I have scored 7.9 CGPA till seventh semester. My hobby is watching movies.

Interviewer: What are reference variables?

Inaas: Reference variables ... I think they are the pointers in C.

Interviewer: Under which chapter, have you studied about them in C?

Inaas: I cannot remember now. We studied it in first year.

Interviewer: And in which year did you study C++?

Inaas: C++ is not a subject for Electronics students.

Interviewer: But you have mentioned C++ knowledge in your resume!

Inaas: Yes, Sir, I know about it to some extent.

Interviewer: Please write a program that explains the namespace property of C++.

Inaas: Sorry, Sir, I am not getting it right now.

Interviewer: No problem, you can write a program that explains encapsulation or data hiding in C++.

Inaas: OK, Sir.

```
/*************************************************************/
class test
{
public:
        int a;
test(){ a = 5};
};
int main ()
{
test testobject ();
cout << testobject.a;
return 0;
}
/*************************************************************/
```

Interviewer: How does this program explain data hiding?

Inaas: We are using a class. Using a class hides data. Class is the concept for encapsulation and writing any code inside gets that property.

(Interviewer: You make class sound like a magic potion, which if applied to a program hides all the program data ... by the way, let me ask you what it is that gets hidden!)

Interviewer: OK. What actually gets hidden, is it variables or constants?

Inaas: Not sure, Sir.

Interviewer: What is happening here: test()

Inaas: test() function is called …

Interviewer: How is C++ different from C?

Inaas: Sir, first it uses OOP concepts like encapsulation, which is not there in C. Second, we can declare variables throughout the code, no need to declare everything at the top. Then some functions are also different; most common are cin and cout instead of scanf and printf.

Interviewer: Any idea why the scanf and printf funtions are not being reused in C++?

Inaas: No, Sir.

Interviewer: What will happen if I use a statement like this in a C++ program?

```
int test(45);
```

Inaas: It is calling a function test with an argument 45.

Interviewer: And if I say test is a variable, not a function?

Inaas: Then it will be a compilation error.

Interviewer: What about a statement like this?

```
a = (b=3, b+2);
```

Inaas: This will also give error.

Interviewer: If I tell you that this is a C statement, not C++, then what will happen?

Inaas: Comma is there; I am not sure, Sir.

Interviewer (*pointing to the sample program written by Inaas*): Inaas, tell me honestly, you have managed to copy this code from somewhere but don't understand it at all, isn't it?

Inaas (*embarrassed*): Yes, Sir, I don't have programming experience with C++.

Interviewer: No problem, you should have told me that earlier! What are your favorite subjects?

Inaas: Digital electronics and analog, digital, and mobile communication.

Interviewer: Tell me how are the pressed keys recognized on your mobile phone? How does it know whether A or D is pressed, then how does it recognize B or E?

Inaas: Hmm ...

Interviewer: Any guesses?

Inaas: I think there should be some software.

Interviewer: What do you know about mobile communication?

Inaas: GSM technology for mobile communication consists of a GSM network. The main elements are MS or mobile station, BTS is the base transceiver, BSC is the base station controller, and MSC is the mobile switching center. These elements are arranged as follows:

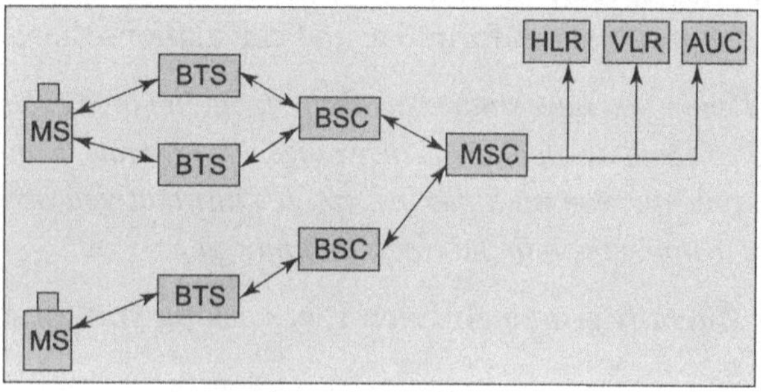

(Interviewer: You draw an intelligent looking diagram but I doubt your awareness of the complexities behind this simplified view.)

Interviewer: Your cell phone works at which frequency?

Inaas: It works in the GSM frequency range.

Interviewer: Does that have any specific value?

Inaas: I think it is near 2 GHz.

Interviewer: How does this system handle roaming customers?

Inaas: It is through HLR and VLR.

Interviewer: That's fine, but how exactly does the process work? Can you draw a flowchart for the steps taken when someone dials a number that is currently on roaming?

Inaas: Sorry, Sir.

Interviewer: Can you give the circuit diagram and working of a successive-approximation-type analog-to-digital converter?

Inaas: Sir, we studied that long back and I cannot remember it now, but I knew it for sure.

Interviewer: Can you tell me why do we face a network jam problem at important moments like the midnight of 31st December, 13th February, etc?

Inaas: Lots of people start making calls but the number of available channels remains fixed. That is the reason the network gets jammed.

Interviewer: That is a correct explanation in a layman's language but quite inadequate one for any engineer. Can you be more specific like what are these channels, how their number is fixed, etc.?

Inaas: I am not sure. Frankly, we don't study subjects like this in electronics. It is more about formulae and calculations there.

(Interviewer: I know you have studied all about it, but in not so explicit a manner. You have studied about available frequency range, Nyquist rate, frequency division multiplexing, time division multiplexing, etc. It's just that you need to use some common sense to apply them to the events around you.)

Interviewer (*literally grinning*): Even I was asking you for a calculation only ☺

Inaas (*smiling sheepishly*): Sir, not like that, we need to know the theorem and formula first.

Interviewer: Let's change the way the discussion is being carried forward. I don't want to ask you a question for which you are unable to provide a satisfactory reply. You pick up topics from the subjects you like and tell me about them. I might ask a related question then.

Inaas: Hmm … topic to talk about … I can tell you about optical fiber communication. It works on the principle of total internal reflection, which takes place when light travels from a denser medium to a rarer medium. The angle of incidence with respect to the denser medium should be greater than the critical angle as per Snell's law. Light traveling in a glass slab might get reflected internally at the glass–air boundary. We see partial bending of light in a prism also.

Optical fibers are made up of a core surrounded by a cladding material. The cladding is a dielectric with a lower refractive index than the core material.

The fiber design can follow one of two types. When the refractive index changes abruptly at the core cladding surface, it is a step index fiber. When the refractive index of the core reduces gradually from the center of the core toward the core boundary, it is called graded index fiber.

Interviewer: When did you study optical fibers?

Inaas: We are studying it in the current semester.

Interviewer: What is the frequency of the light used in optical fiber communication?

Inaas: Frequency ... frequency, no, I am not sure but the 1300–1500 nm wavelength is generally used for this communication.

Interviewer: At this wavelength, it should be called as ultraviolet communication, not optical communication! Is that right?

Inaas: Not sure of that, Sir.

Interviewer: Leave it then! Please continue on to another topic now.

Inaas: Another topic is flip-flop. A flip-flop is a sequential circuit. It acts as a memory element as long as power remains on. It is a sequential circuit as the output is tied to the input and the output at any time depends on the previous output value. NAND and NOR gates are used in flip-flop design.

Flip-flops can be of type RS, JK, D, and T. A flip-flop is defined by its characteristic table. For example, the T flip-flop's table shows that whenever T is made high, the output toggles from its previous state.

Q	T	Q (t + 1)
0	0	0
0	1	1
1	0	1
1	1	0

For JK flip-flop, the characteristic table ...

Interviewer: That's enough for flip-flop!

Inaas: I know C concepts like recursion, pointers, arrays, structures, macros, etc. I will explain them one by one.

Interviewer: That would be too much of a trouble for you. Just explain the macro concept.

Inaas: Macros are preprocessor directives and are executed before compilation. They are used for making C programs readable and easy to use.

For example,

1. We have to use "pi" value with a four decimal digits in the code. Instead of keying in all the seven characters and making a mistake in the actual value, we may want to use the name PI everywhere. Then we can define PI as a macro.

```
#define PI 3.1428
```

2. We have to calculate area of a trapezium many times and we don't want to use a function for that. Then the formula can be defined as a macro.

```
#define AREA(X,Y,Z) (0.5 * ((X)+(Y)) * (Z))
```

Then AREA(1,2,3) can be called just like a function anywhere in the code. Macros are substituted like a string wherever they are used in a program, so it is good to use brackets when using macros for expressions.

We can also test if a macro is defined or not by using "#ifdef macro name" or "#ifndef macro name."

Interviewer: That's very interesting!

Inaas: Yes, Sir. Another interesting concept is compiler boot strapping. If a C compiler code is written in C itself, that is, if the compiler source code is written in the same language which has to be compiled by the compiled compiler code, then it is known as compiler bootstrapping.

Anyways, bootstrapping is a very frequently used concept in computers. Like a bootstrap loader is used to load the OS into memory when a PC is powered on, etc.

Interviewer: A wonderful concept indeed! I am done with asking you questions. Do you have any for me?

Inaas: No, Sir.

Interviewer: Very good then!

Inaas: Thanks, Sir.

SCENE 3

The interviewer is in a state of utter dilemma. After dillydallying for half an hour and finishing one more interview, he finally gives his partial feedback on Inaas.

Discipline Knowledge – Acceptable.

Computers Knowledge – C Basics Acceptable

Communication – Good

Comments – Inaas has a lot of bookish knowledge but lacks in application knowledge.

Result -

SCENE 4

The interviewer is still not able to fill in the result section. In the heart of his heart, he does not want to mark him as a select. He knows he has rejected better students at other institutes. But here the situation has been dismal till now. Students' level has been found a lot below expectations. Inaas is certainly privileged against this backdrop. After all, a one-eyed man is the king in the country of blind. But he does not want to take such a subjective decision by himself. Thus he meets up with Coder's campus manager.

Interviewer: There is this candidate Inaas and I am confused about him. Personally, I don't want to select him as his application knowledge is at a very poor level.

Campus Manager: Then what is stopping you from rejecting him outright?

Interviewer: His marks! He has been a consistent performer with a distinction score always. He also happens to be the one who topped our written test and that too with a huge margin!

Campus Manager: Ahh, I get that now! How is he at communication?

Interviewer: Quite good.

Campus Manager: How bad is he at tech?

Interviewer: He had mentioned C++ in his CV and I started asking him questions on that. I don't remember if he could answer any. It took me a while to realize that it was mentioned just for the impression purpose! He could have owned that up earlier, which he did only when I asked him directly.

After that, the discussion veered toward his discipline and I discovered that theoretically speaking he is good. He knows a lot of stuff he has studied and can recite it beautifully. The problem lies in correlating it with the events around. He knows the layman's reason why a network gets busy when lot of people try calling but cannot tell how this "lot of people" count can be derived! He knows optical fiber communication concepts but cannot tell the light frequency as it is traveling inside the cable. I am sure he must have separately studied the physics concept that frequency remains the same and the wavelength changes but has never seen a mention of frequency in optic fiber chapters, so could not answer quickly.

Campus Manager: Does that mean if I pick up such questions from Google that I don't understand much, his replies would sound convincing enough to me?

Interviewer: Definitely.

Campus Manager: Personally, I do give a chance to such students.

Interviewer: Hmm ... Let me also give him a chance then and mark him as a Select!

❋ ❋ ❋

16

MCA's Ved Appears for Drive Automations

SCENE 1

Drive Automations is not a regular IT company. They build software for vehicles and are known to offer a very good package and pick the best of the students. Getting an offer from them is a privilege every student dreams of. Ved has consulted two of his seniors who were picked by DA in the previous years and has been advised to be true to himself and use common sense. Given the hype around their interview process, any amount of counseling cannot help him and he is still anxious about his performance.

SCENE 2

Interviewer: You are Ved, right?

Ved: Hello Sir; yes.

Interviewer: What is your educational background?

Ved: Sir, I passed class XII from CBSE, Science stream, with 84 percent marks in 2006. After that I did BSc in computer Science from Delhi University in 2009 and topped the university in my discipline. The very same year I joined this institute to pursue MCA.

Interviewer: Which all languages are you comfortable with?

Ved: C, C++, Java, Pascal, SQL, PL/SQL.

(Interviewer: Listing programming languages and not spoken languages is a good omen for you.)

Interviewer: Are you sure you have written a decent amount of PL/SQL-based code?

Ved: Yes, Sir, I have used it in one of our projects.

Interviewer: Can you write a procedure that you have written for your project?

Ved: Yes, Sir. We had done one project for implementing a data mining system for the local store Parivesh here. We had developed a screen for customer billing. As a part of the screen code, a procedure UpdateSales was written for calculating total sales. This store wanted to keep the retail customer sales and business customer sales separate. Business customers included local hospitals, security agencies, etc., who ordered dresses from them. I will write down this procedure again now.

```
/* SECTION 1 *********************************************/

CREATE OR REPLACE PROCEDURE UpdateSales
(CustomerName IN CUSTOMER_DETAIL.CUSTOMER_NAME%TYPE,
GroupName IN CUSTOMER_DETAIL.GROUP_NAME%TYPE,
sqlMessage OUT VARCHAR2)

IS

/* SECTION 2 *********************************************/

varCount INTEGER;

CURSOR cCustomer IS

SELECT UPPER(D.CUSTOMER_NAME), D.SALES, D. SEQ_NUM,
M.GROUP_CODE, M.CUSTOMER_ID
FROM CUSTOMER_DETAIL D, CUSTOMER_MASTER M
```

```
    WHERE D.CUSTOMER_NAME = CustomerName
AND D.CUSTOMER_NAME = M.CUSTOMER_NAME
AND D.GROUP_NAME = GroupName
    AND D.GROUP_NAME = M.GROUP_NAME
AND D.PROCESSED_FLAG IS NULL

/* SECTION 3 *******************************************/

BEGIN
sqlMessage := ' Procedure UpdateSales Completed Successfully ';

FOR i .. N cCustomer LOOP                                   --3.1
    IF i.GROUP_CODE = 1 THEN                                --3.2

        SELECT COUNT(*) FROM RETAIL_SALES                   --3.3
        WHERE CUSTOMER_ID = i.CUSTOMER_ID into varCount;

        IF varCount > 0 THEN                                --3.3

            UPDATE RETAIL_SALES A                           --3.4
            SET RETAIL_SALES =  A.RETAIL_SALES + i.SALES
            WHERE CUSTOMER_ID = i.CUSTOMER_ID;
        ELSE                                                --3.4
            INSERT INTO RETAIL_SALES(CUSTOMER_ID, RETAIL_SALES)
            VALUES(i.CUSTOMER_ID, i.SALES)
        END IF;
    ELSE

        SELECT COUNT(*) FROM BUSINESS_SALES
        WHERE CUSTOMER_NAME = i.CUSTOMER_NAME into varCount;

        IF varCount > 0 THEN
```

```
            UPDATE BUSINESS_SALES A
            SET BUSINESS_SALES =  A.BUSINESS_SALES + i.SALES
            WHERE CUSTOMER_NAME = i.CUSTOMER_NAME
        ELSE
            INSERT INTO BUSINESS_SALES
            (CUSTOMER_NAME, BUSINESS_SALES)
            VALUES(i.CUSTOMER_NAME, i.SALES)
        END IF;
    END IF;

    UPDATE CUSTOMER_DETAIL SET PROCESSED_FLAG = 'Y'        –3.5
WHERE UPPER(CUSTOMER_NAME) = i.CUSTOMER_NAME
AND GROUP_NAME = GroupName
AND SEQ_NUM = i.SEQ_NUM

END LOOP;

COMMIT;

/* SECTION 4 ********************************************/

EXCEPTION

WHEN OTHERS THEN
    sqlMessage := (' Error encountered in Procedure UpdateSales : ' ||
SUBSTR(SQLERRM,1,1024));

END;
/*******************************************************/
```

Interviewer: Please explain these sections one by one.

Ved:

In section 1, the procedure is created with three input parameters and one output parameter. The input parameters get the value from the screen code procedure call. The syntax for parameter is "ParameterName ParameterType DataType."

```
CustomerName IN CUSTOMER_DETAIL.CUSTOMER_NAME%TYPE,
```

This implies that the parameter name is CustomerName, type is IN or input, and the data type for this parameter is same as the data type defined for the field CUSTOMER_NAME in the CUSTOMER_DETAIL table.

In section 2, a cursor "cCustomer" is defined to fetch the matching data from the CUSTOMER tables through an inner join on …

Interviewer: Move over to the next section please.

Ved:

In section 3,

3.1. The records are read one by one in the cursor for loop through the cursor variable "i." It behaves like a temporary table with a single record.

3.2. Then we check if the record belongs to a retail customer or business customer. The if-else logic is similar to C except that we need to include an END IF statement. This is understood as we do not use curly braces here, so compiler has no way of knowing where the clause ends.

3.3 After this we decide whether to update the sales value of an existing record or to insert the new customer record in the RETAIL_SALES or BUSINESS_SALES table. This is done by checking for the existence of a record with the same key value.

3.4 After this, the corresponding insert statement or update statement is fired. We add the cursor sales value to the current sales value to get the new sales total.

3.5 After this, the CUSTOMER_DETAIL table record is marked as processed.

Section 4 captures any error encountered and sets a return message with the corresponding error message. "||" is used for concatenation. "SQLERRM" stores the system-generated error message.

(Interviewer: Ved, you have raised my expectations from you to a very high level by this thorough explanation. I know you have missed most of the semicolons, but that is certainly forgivable.)

Interviewer: What is method overriding in Java?

Ved: If a method with same name and type are defined in both a superclass and its subclass and the method is called from the subclass reference, then it is always the version of the subclass method that is called. The superclass method cannot be called directly. Thus a subclass method hides a superclass method and this characteristic is called as method overriding. Overriding happens in case of class data members also.

Interviewer: In this situation, is it possible to call the superclass member in any way?

Ved: Yes, calling the method as super.method name will refer to the method in the super class.

Interviewer: Have a look at the following program and tell me what will be the output if I assure that it will compile fine?

```
/*************************************************************/
class A {
        void test() {
        System.out.println("Class A");}}
class B extends A {
void test() {
System.out.println("Class B");}
        public static void main(){
B Cobj = new B();
                Cobj.test();}}
class C extends B {
        void test() {
                System.out.println("Class C");
                super.test();}
        public static void main(String args[]){
                C Cobj = new C();
                Cobj.main();
```

```
            Cobj.test();}
    public static void main(){
            A Cobj = new A();
            Cobj.test();
            B Bobj = new B();
            Bobj.main();}}
/***********************************************************/
```

Ved (*perplexed after looking at the program for a minute*): It looks a bit complicated, Sir …

Interviewer: So you will avoid all complicated-looking assignments at work?

Ved (*digesting the demeaning remark with a suppressed smile*): Not really, I would want to take it. Please give me a few minutes; let me analyze the flow and mark it.

Interviewer: I am fine as long as the "few" remains a single-digit number!

Ved (*with allayed tension*): Thanks, Sir!

(Ved: It is confusing and I should start from the main, but which main. It is overloaded in class C and it is overridden with respect to classes B and C. Oh got the tail, let me pull this beast by the tail now! The class C version with String array argument is the one to start with; let me mark it as 1.

Then it calls C.main(), the overloaded main with no arguments; mark it as 2.

Then it calls A.test(), which prints "Class A." The object variable names don't have much role to play as there does not seem to be much of a conflict except that they are also overridden.. Control comes back to C.main() and calls the otherwise overridden B.main(). B.test() is called next to print "Class B." C.main() is done, yippie! Control is back at the third statement of C.main(String).

It calls C.test, which prints "Class C" and then calls the test() method from its immediate superclass, that is, B.test(). It prints "Class B" again. Looks like I can be rechristened as "The JVM" now!

By the way, let me explain it to my not-so-friendly angel before my time is over!)

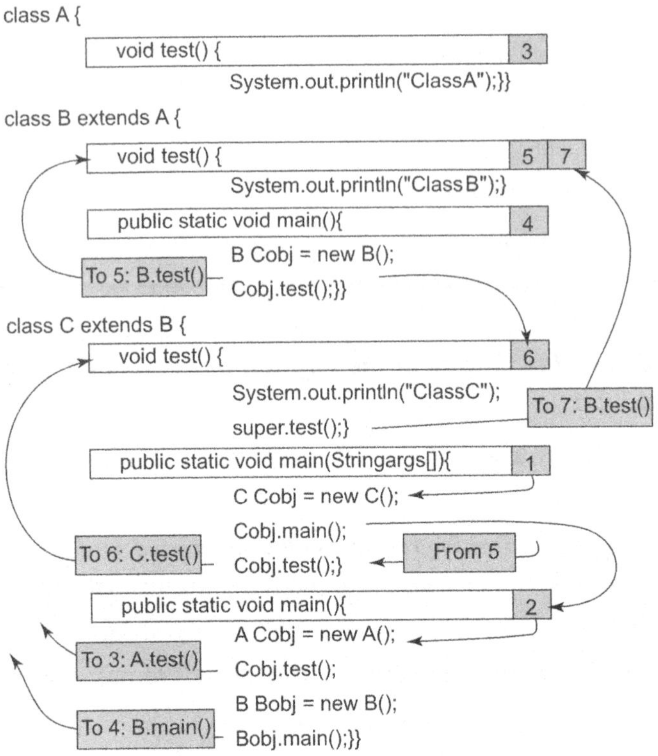

Ved (*with allayed tension*): Sir, going by the flow as I have marked on the paper, the output looks like this:

Class A

Class B

Class C

Class B

(The interviewer who had been keenly watching Ved trace the flow is impressed by his impeccable work but he does not believe in sharing his feelings with the interviewees as that might make them comfortable and casual!)

Interviewer: How confident are you that it will generate the same output if I run it on my laptop right now?

Ved (*a bit unnerved and defensive*): I am confident, Sir.

Interviewer: How much? Can you define your confidence as a percentage?

Ved (*quite aggressive*): Give me one more minute please, Sir.

(Ved quickly works his way through the program.)

Sir, going by the initial assumption that there are no compilation-related errors, I am 100 percent confident of the output.

(Interviewer: Smart boy, you did remember and refer to the initial assumption! You would be a definite select if you would endure the stress till the end and not crack in between!)

Interviewer (*feigning sarcasm to maintain high stress level*): You look over-confident and that's not supposed to be very good! What is a constructor?

Ved: It is a Java concept used to create a physical copy of the object in the memory. It is used in conjunction with the "new" keyword. When a constructor is called, physical memory is allotted class data members and these memory locations are assigned the initial values for these data members. This is the reason it is called constructor. For example, a class DemoConstructor is written as follows:

```
/*************************************************************/
class DemoConstructor
{       int a;
        boolean b;
        char c;
        double d;

        DemoConstructor(){}
}
class test
{       public static void main(String[] args)
        {       DemoConstructor check = new DemoConstructor();
                System.out.println(check.a +" "+ check.b +" "+ check.c +" "+
check.d);
        }}
/*************************************************************/
```

Here the constructor DemoConstructor() creates a reference of the same class type and assigns it to the check object. It also initializes the variables a, b, c, and d to values 0, false, 00, and 0.0, respectively. This constructor is behaving like the default constructor that Java creates in case no constructor is defined.

Interviewer: Can you prove that the constructor return type is same as the class?

Ved: Yes, Sir. In the above program, if we modify the print statement like this:

```
System.out.println((check + 1));
```

The program will fail to compile. The compile error will show the type of check as "DemoConstructor."

Interviewer: Can we apply the varargs concept to constructors?

Ved: varargs allows us to pass variable number of arguments to a function in the form of implicit array elements, very similar to the manner main(String[] args). I am not sure if the same holds true for constructor argument passing. But logically speaking, it should be possible to do so.

Interviewer: Assume that is supported and there are four variables a, b, c, and d that have to be initialized through a constructor. It is necessary to initialize "a." Others are optional parameters. Can you write the constructor for this?

Ved: Yes, Sir, we can handle this through constructor overloading. I can ...

Interviewer: I said a single constructor definition using the varargs concept.

Ved: I have not handled it for constructors; please give me some time to think about it.

(Ved's brain is working at a feverish pitch. He tries to replicate the variable arguments function style for the constructor and settles for a switch case statement. But he does not like the original version of the code where he needs to reassign values to all the variables inside every option. He decides to use an extra variable "i" to avoid this repetition and ends up scribbling a decent code. The interviewer asks him for explanation and he marks the important parts with explanation.)

```
/*************************************************************/
class VariableArgs
{   int a, b, c, d, i = 0;
    VariableArgs(intx, int... y)   → Intx accepts required arg, array y accepts optional args
    {   a = x;                     → x is assigned to a
        for (int z : y )           → Read elements from array y one by one into z
        {   switch (i)
            {   case 0:
                    b = y[i];          → 0th element is assigned to b
                case 1:
                    if (1 > i) break;  → Break if no more args
                    c = y[i];          → 1st element is assigned to c
                case 2:
                    if (2 > i) break;
                    d = y[i];
                default: break;
            } i++;
        }
    }
}
public static void main(String[] args)
{       VariableArgs check = new VariableArgs(5,10,15,20);}

/*************************************************************/
```

Interviewer: What will happen if I add one more constructor to your code?

```
VariableArgs(int m, int n, int ... x) {}
```

Ved: It will fail to resolve the constructor call as the type signature for both of these constructors matches in this case. It will generate a compile-time error.

Interviewer: All right. That's all I had to ask. You may now leave.

Ved: Good day, Sir!

SCENE 3

After coming out of the interview room, Ved suddenly feels very tired. No amount of prior information could prepare him to face such a stern interviewer. He is coaxed by others for the asked questions. He mentions that he was asked a lot of questions and starts recounting them, "I was asked about stored procedures, constructors, varargs, method overriding ... what else, OMG, I was asked just four questions! I had to write code for all of them and that consumed time." This sudden realization about the miniscule number of questions sends a chill down his spine and makes him even more uncertain about the outcome.

SCENE 4

The interviewer is pleased to find a third select in a single day as it makes his overall workload lesser! He fills in the detailed form used for Campus Selects and assigns Ved the highest ratings for this season.

Rating

Technical Knowledge – 7.5/10

Stress Management Skills – 8/10

Programming Aptitude – 8.5/10

Common Sense – 8/10

Justification

Technical Knowledge – Ved answered 90–95 percent of the technical questions correctly. For a couple of situations, where he did not know the answer upfront, he guessed a correct answer and substantiated the reply with a logical explanation. He was not confused on any of the concepts even when made a bit tensed. He stood by his answers even when I tried to sow seeds of suspicion over the accuracy in his mind. All this speaks well about his technical depth.

Stress Management Skills – He appeared at ease most of the time and nasty remarks could not agitate him visibly. He concentrated on the topic of discussion throughout the interview even though he was not provided any hint on his overall performance any time during the discussion. He did not require my assistance to pull him out of tough situations. On top of that, he could retain his cool and could think of cool logic for the given problems.

Programming Aptitude – He wrote syntactically correct and logically coherent programs for questions not found in college books and could even improvise well on draft versions within a reasonable timeframe. Most of the code written by him did not conform to the age-old lengthy programs written by students and displayed many instances of fresh logic. Still, it was easy to get an understanding of the logic by simply seeing him develop it.

Common Sense – He has completed many projects including one for a real customer. The field situations needed him to apply common sense on deciding on the technologies to be used and segregate implementation in a front-end and a back-end component. He took care to ensure that the two layers could communicate easily and back-end-related problems could be displayed in a user-friendly manner on the front-end. Being able to apply such learned concepts to solve a real-time problem definitely calls for common sense.

17

Electrical's Manav and Invensys Corp

SCENE 1

Manav firmly believes in the adages "man is a mere actor" and "whatever has to happen will happen." Unlike other students he is not rushing through notes at the last minute. Rather he is observing the activity around him with keen interest as it has provided him a chance to study authentic myriad emotions quickly. He is thinking of composing a humorous poem on the drama called company visit and is tempted to jot down the initial lines. He is called as he is penning his thoughts.

SCENE 2

Interviewer: Hey Manav, how are you?

Manav: Hi Sir, I am fine.

Interviewer: What is going to be the result of this interview, what do you think?

Manav (*taken aback*): Sir … sir … not sure …

Interviewer: Do you have no confidence in yourself?

Manav: Not like that, but it will depend …

Interviewer: Depend on what?

Manav: Hmm …

Interviewer: Hmm?

Manav: Depend on questions!

Interviewer: How will it depend on questions of all the things?

Manav: Whether the questions are from subjects I know or …

Interviewer: Let me make things easier for you then. You have to tell me about the subjects you are comfortable with and I will question you on those subjects only. Does that sound good to you?

Manav (*delighted*): Yes, yes.

Interviewer: How comfortable are you with your minor and major project?

Manav: I am comfortable.

Interviewer: Explain your minor project.

Manav (*opening the project report and referring to the index*): In this project, we have …

Interviewer: Close this file please and give a general overview.

Manav: This is a sunflower project. Like a sunflower rotates to keep facing the sun, we can rotate a solar panel to keep on facing the sun always. We have done the project to do this.

Interviewer: Have you heard of Pranav Mistry? I believe he is the one to ideate this concept!

Manav: Not much, Sir; we thought of it before him actual …

Interviewer (*as if smacked on face*): Oh really? What do you know about him? What is he doing?

Manav: He … hmm

Interviewer (*miffed*): Don't forget to look at pranavmistry.com after the interview then!

Manav: OK.

Interviewer (*sarcastically*): Back to "your" sunflower project, how has it been done?

Manav: The panel had to rotate by some degrees every hour. To find the value was very difficult. We had to test it out in the sun for many days to get the right values for rotation degree.

Interviewer: How could you rotate the huge solar panel by a few degrees every hour?

Manav: We did not use a solar panel, but mounted an A4-size Thermocol sheet.

Interviewer: That's fine; how could you move the sheet then?

Manav: We used a motor for that.

Interviewer: What type of motor? How many degrees per hour?

Manav: I don't remember the actual value for degrees. The motor was a DC motor.

Interviewer: What type of DC motor?

Manav: ?

Interviewer: Was it a stepper motor?

Manav: Yes, Sir, a stepper motor.

Interviewer: Can you give me all the calculations you used for determining the motor step size?

Manav: ...

Interviewer: How did you send the right signal waveforms to the motor at the right intervals of an hour each?

Manav: You are asking about power supply?

Interviewer: No, I was talking about the microcontroller code that you might have used! I am curious what happened to your sunflower once it was night.

Manav: I did not get that, Sir?

Interviewer: What did it do at night? How did it stop rotating at night? How did it achieve the correct orientation the next morning after having turned almost 180 degrees the previous evening?

Manav: Not sure, Sir; we did not test it like that.

Interviewer: I want you to talk to me in "I" terms. Tell me which part of the project was done by you and you only and not by your team?

Manav: It is ... it is not like that, we have done all the work together as it was minor project and we were only three in a group.

(Interviewer: Well, Manav, you are a gone case! It's a pain I have to kill another five minutes with you, does not look good if I reject students in under five minutes' timeframe!)

Interviewer: What have you done for your major project?

Manav: In the major project, we are designing a system for detecting power theft.

Interviewer: What do you mean by that?

Manav: We see that people steal power from OHT lines by hanging wires on the cables and taking these wires to their houses. We are doing a circuit that can detect this.

(Interviewer: This city seems to be blessed with a project messiah who is doing really interesting work; only if these dumb students cared to understand any of the stuff they bought from him!)

Interviewer: Hmm ...

Manav: A difference circuit is inserted between two target nodes to identify any loads on the lines between the nodes. I will draw the circuit diagram to explain that.

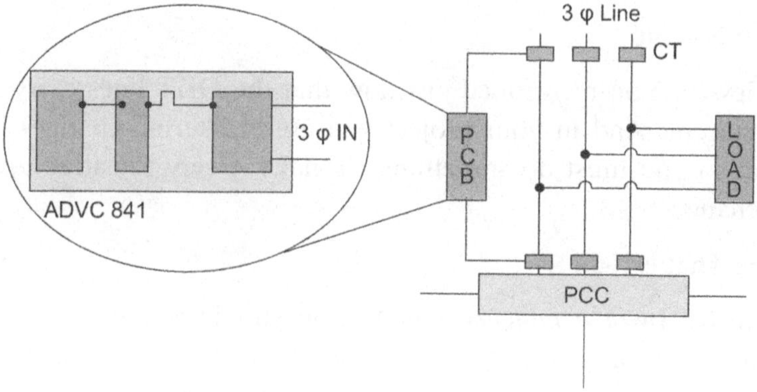

(Interviewer: You have lost your chance and cannot impress me with a complicated looking diagram. I am definitely going to validate your cognizance of this circuit!)

Interviewer: How did you test this circuit? How could you feed a three-phase supply to this circuit?

Manav: Electrical labs have a three-phase connection at all the work tables; we connected to the same.

Interviewer: What did you measure between the two nodes, current difference or voltage difference?

Manav: Current change.

Interviewer: How could you check that? There might be legitimate customers also and you cannot really determine a current difference. Current will also fluctuate when such customers consume varying loads!

Manav (*puzzled*): We did not consider that, I think.

Interviewer: Why is that OHT is done at such high voltages only and not lower voltages?

Manav: It is to avoid heat losses in the line.

Interviewer: How is the heat loss prevented?

Manav: V = IR. "I" decreases when "V" is increased. This also reduces a lot of heat loss, as loss = IR^2.

Interviewer: What is the current sensitivity of your project circuit?

Manav: ...

Interviewer: Do you understand why am I asking that?

Manav: No, Sir.

Interviewer: You mentioned just now that the OHT lines carry a very small current. And in your project you are measuring changes in that current, so you must do something to make it very sensitive to detect small changes.

Manav: That is right ...

Interviewer (*with a naughty smile*): You should ask the guy who is developing this project for you to take all these things into consideration now. It will be easier for you to face the project viva. ☺

Manav (*thoroughly embarrassed*): Sir, I will study the project in more detail now.

Interviewer: That will also help you perform better in the next interview!

Manav (*dismayed*): Sir, you won't select me?

Interviewer (*jolted at such a direct question*): What would have you done if you were in my place?

Manav: Sir, I know C and I can answer questions from power systems and machines. Can you please ask me questions on that?

Interviewer (*feeling guilty and avoiding a direct no*): See, your other friends are waiting for their turns. Let me see if I have some time after I have finished talking to them!

Manav (*hopeful*): Sir, please consider my request.

Interviewer: Let me see that, Manav. But do keep in mind that I am not committing anything to you!

Manav (*dispirited*): Thank you Sir.

SCENE 3

Manav is torn between two conflicting thoughts. One part of his brain wants to pray for a second-round interview while the other part is highly skeptical about talking to an interviewer who digs a lot. Unable to cope with the surmounting tension, he stops thinking and simply waits for the next event. At the same time, the interviewer sends his verdict:

Result – Tech Reject

Technical Knowledge – Not Acceptable

Computer Knowledge – Not checked.

Attitude – Not Acceptable

SCENE 4

The HR coordinator is not happy on seeing that his favorite placement team volunteer has been rejected. He requests the interviewer to reconsider his decision on Manav. The interviewer refuses. The HR requests again. The interviewer does not budge. The HR mentions that Manav had been really active, he had communicated with him on mail also regarding the event, and should be given some credit for that.

The interviewer challenges him, "let me narrate what happened and then see if your high opinion about him remains unchanged!

He has copied his sunflower project idea from a famous inventor's work but does not know anything about him. On top of that he lies that he was the first one to get that idea; I could see it very clearly that he has not done the project by himself, but has rather bought it. It is such a famous concept and if it had been a reinvention, he would have definitely searched for past implementations and got a reference of the guy. In fact he could have implemented it in a much better way than what he has bought now. I would have been absolutely fine with the buying part if he had even tried to understand how it was done and had not lied so blatantly.

Another point, it's good to say 'we' have done so and so, it shows you can work well with a group, but it is not good not to do anything and then hide your indolence behind the group; I would also be interested in knowing what has been the individual's contribution to the project. I need to be sure that the candidate is going to be an asset, not a burden to his team.

Engineering aptitude is poor. I could pick out questions on his project within a few minutes even though I am from a different discipline. Surprising to see that he could not think of any of those! He does know some basic theory. But if that were sufficient, we would have been conducting a subjective test and not really flying down so many people to gain an insight on the technical prowess of these students.

Now tell me, would you want to take him into your team? By the way, don't forget 'that humongous lie'. I see that as an attitude problem."

The HR loses the challenge.

***

18

MCA's Roshni and Speak Up Systems

SCENE 1

Roshni has been completing her final-semester internship with a small but demanding company and had a tough time getting three days off for the campus event. Their argument is that when they have already offered her a position, what is the need to look out further. On the other hand, Roshni wants to commence her career with a company with a bigger name. She is desperate to get through this event to avoid making further excuses for leaves. Another reason is that Speak Up Systems does not ask for any commitment from students on a bond paper!

SCENE 2

Roshni: Good morning, Sir.

Interviewer: Good morning, Roshni. Which are your favorite subjects?

Roshni: DBMS, Software Engineering, and Java.

Interviewer: Explain the differences between 1NF, 2NF, and 3NF.

Roshni: A table in 1NF form has no duplicate data across rows or columns. The rows are identified with a primary key.

A 2NF table fulfills the 1NF requirement. In addition to this, all data redundancies are removed by moving related data in separate 1NF tables. For example, instead of storing the address fields for all customers in the customer table, a separate table for address is created. These two tables are joined through a primary and foreign key relationship. Here AddressID might be the primary key in the address table and become the foreign key in the customer table.

A 3NF fulfills 2NF requirements. Additionally, all the fields not dependent on the primary key are taken out of the table and put in a separate table, if needed.

(In the meanwhile, the interviewer has created a table on a sheet of paper.)

Interviewer (*pointing to the table*): Have a look at this table given below and normalize it as much as you can.

Student_Name	Subject 1	Subject 2	Marks 1	Marks 2
Akshat	Compiler Design	Processor Architecture	65	71
Cyrus	Neural Network	Artificial Intelligence	54	76
Saranya	Compiler Design	Processor Architecture	56	82
Tarun	Web Technologies	Network Security	79	65
Vishesh	Web Technologies	Network Security	85	75

(Roshni: There are three subject areas, students, subjects, and marks, and I should segregate these into three tables. Marks would be the main table in the 3NF form; I need to introduce codes for the primary key purpose. It will easily become a 3NF model now. Let me draw the tables now.)

Roshni: Sir, this table can be normalized into a 3NF form. There is no duplication of data; primary keys are defined. Relationships based on the primary keys are also defined. STUDENT_ID is primary key for STUDENT table, SUBJECT_CODE for SUBJECT table, and composite key STUDENT_ID and SUBJECT_CODE is for the MARKS table. For the MARKS table, STUDENT_ID is also a foreign key field and it depends on the STUDENT table. SUBJECT_CODE is another foreign key dependent on the SUBJECT table.

STUDENT

Student_ID■	Student_Name
1	Akshat
2	Cyrus
3	Saranya
4	Tarun
5	Vishesh

SUBJECT

Subject_Code■	Subject
S11	Compiler design
S12	Neural Network
S13	Web Technologies
S21	Processor Architecture
S22	Artificial Intelligence
S23	Network Security

MARKS

Student_ID■	Subject_Code■	Marks
1	S11	65
1	S21	71
2	S12	54
2	S22	76
3	S11	56
3	S21	82
4	S13	79
4	S23	65
5	S13	85
5	S23	75

Interviewer: Good! What are the various software lifecycle process models that you have studied?

Roshni: We have studied about the waterfall model, which is the main or basic model. There are incremental and evolutionary models also. We were just introduced to the agile model but it was not included in detail.

Interviewer: Hmm, what is the waterfall model?

Roshni: It is the classic software development lifecycle process and it specifies a systematic and sequential approach to software development. The first phase in this model is the requirements phase where the customer specifies the requirements for which he plans to get the software developed. We discuss these requirements with the customer to get a deeper understanding. Next phase is the planning phase. Technology-related decision making, estimation, and project activity scheduling are done.

This is followed by the modeling or the design phase, where the technical blueprint for the software application is developed.

In the construction phase, which comes next, the actual code is developed based on the design and then tested.

This is followed by application deployment and the customer starts using the application.

Interviewer: You sound pretty well versed; do you have any application development experience following this model?

Roshni: Yes, Sir. We were given a project to develop an application for digital image processing in the last semester and our guide instructed us to follow all the phases properly. The guide acted as the customer for the project. In this semester, I am doing internship with MBCL Soft. They are following this approach in the project there also. We are in the construction phase right now, but when I had joined, the project was in design phase. My mentors explained to me documents from the earlier two phases also. They are very strict; all the major milestone deadlines have been put up at all the cubicles there. In fact, I don't feel like an intern but a full-time employee there.

Interviewer: What type of work do you do there?

Roshni: I am supposed to write Java code but I am able to do that for maximum three days of the week. For the other three days, dirty data creation and manual testing work is assigned to me by the testing team seniors. But when I talk to my classmates, I realize that I have done a lot more coding than them and learnt a lot more as well. I am happy that way.

Interviewer: Did you say you work six days a week?

Roshni: Yes, Sir.

Interviewer: You must be getting a good stipend then, isn't it?

Roshni: No, Sir. They say students should pay them for getting live project experience; ultimately no one pays the other.

Interviewer: Why did you choose to work with them then?

Roshni: It is the only company in my hometown which accepted an internship request. I wanted to stay at home for some time. It's different that I am not getting to do that now anyways.

Interviewer: Why do you want to join us then?

Roshni: Sir, Speak Up Systems is a big brand name. It is also known as a company which gives very good training and allocates fresher students to good projects. These are the reasons why I dream of joining SUS.

Interviewer: You look trained quite well already! What type of code do you need to write?

Roshni: My current assignment is to write applets for five of the customer requirements.

Interviewer: Can you elaborate on the requirements?

Roshni: Sure, Sir. Our customer is a bank coaching institute and they plan to build a portal for letting students decide on the type of course they want to join. Right now, their office has to handle a lot of queries from students on a daily basis, who want to know how much they will have to spend if they join a particular combination of training module and test series.

For this purpose, they want to include a section on their website where the student can have a look at all the possible options and then select a particular combination to see how much it will cost him. Basically, they want that the office attends to only the registered students, not to others who come every now and then to get information on course cost.

I am working on this requirement right now.

Interviewer: Sounds interesting. What are the basic things I need to know before I can write any applet?

Roshni: Sir, Java package java.applet provides a class Applet. Any of the applets created will be a subclass of Applet. This class provides the important methods init(), start(), and paint() …

Actually, sorry Sir, paint() is provided by awt package. So this package needs to be imported in the applet code as well.

An applet does not need to include a main() function as it is run by a browser generally based on any event on the web page, as is the case with our project.

Parameters can also be passed to the applets, which is also something that I am doing.

Interviewer: All right Roshni, as a last question, you can tell me anything on Java that you want to and which has not been discussed till now.

Roshni: I can tell about access modifiers. "Public," "private," "protected," and default or no modifiers can be used to restrict access to Java objects.

When a member is declared as public, it can be called from anywhere within or outside its class. "main()" method is an example. There is absolutely no restriction on its access.

A private member displays just the opposite characteristics. Its access scope is limited to the class in which it is defined. It is not accessible from inner classes or subclasses also. It's strictly restricted to its class.

A protected member can be accessed from anywhere within its package. From outside its package, it can be accessed from subclasses only.

A default scope is package-level scope. So a default access member can be accessed from anywhere within its package but not from anywhere at all outside its package.

Interviewer: Fine, Roshni! You will be getting a call for the HR round soon.

Roshni (*pleasantly surprised*): Thanks, Sir.

SCENE 3

As Roshni waits for the next-round call, the interviewer fills the feedback form.

Technical Knowledge – Very Good at DB, Java, understands SE concepts.

Project Description – Very Good; she has a live project experience, too.

Communication – Quite clear, effortless, spontaneous.

Roshni is marked as a Tech Select.

SCENE 4

Speak Up Systems follows the policy of letting the interviewers recommend any exceptional students they discovered for positions a notch higher than what is generally offered to the regular students. The interviewer decides to recommend one student.

I recommend Roshni for the exceptional students track. She has a stronghold on concepts and displayed that in solving the given problems. She is also very spontaneous at communication.

In addition to this, she has worked on a customer-facing project and understands the SDLC concepts and her role quite well. She is a genuine candidate who displayed a lot of maturity in discussing her work. She has learnt to take time to understand and evaluate the given situation before jumping on to coding, a trait usually not seen in freshers.

She can be considered as one with around a year of IT experience already though she has been into internship for few months only. Based on her present level of maturity at software application development, she is fit to take up a challenging role and need not be spoon-fed.

* * *

19

MTech's Naveen and Globe Printers Hurdle

SCENE 1

Naveen has got a job with an environmental agency but he wants to try his luck at an IT job also. GP conducts direct interviews for students clearing the written test. That's why it is considered an easy company. Naveen has devised a strategy to emphasize on the software he has seen or used in the lab to make him appear more suitable.

SCENE 2

Interviewer: Hi Naveen, have a seat please.

Naveen (*clumsily pulling the chair*): Yes, yes Sir.

Interviewer: Tell me about your hostel life.

Naveen: Hostel life is good. We go out or talk with others or watch TV, like that only.

Interviewer: You are pursuing MTech from which subject?

Naveen: Sir, I am doing in GIS and remote sensing.

Interviewer: Can I please see your CV?

Naveen (*handing out the CV*): Yes, Sir.

Interviewer: Do you know C?

Naveen: Yes, C basics.

Interviewer: Do you know anything else in computers?

Naveen: No, Sir.

Interviewer: How will you work in IT then?

Naveen: We use many software in GIS. I feel comfortable in that.

Interviewer: That is fine, then. Let's talk about your project now.

Naveen: Sir, my project is location-based service project. I am creating map of our institute. There are two modules in that:

1. User module
2. C2S module

In user module, using GPS to calculate coordinates (x,y) for geo-reference map. In second module, map server used for navigation map…

Interviewer: Let me see if I understood you correctly till now. Do you mean to say, you are creating a digital map of your institute campus and using GPS for the same?

Naveen: Yes.

Interviewer: Why are you doing it like this? There must be hundreds of paper maps available for your campus. Why don't you simply digitize them?

Naveen: We doing environment analysis for tourism also, that's why.

Interviewer (*amused*): You plan to develop your campus as a tourist hot spot?

Naveen: That is, we doing for the city.

Interviewer: OK.

Naveen: For that, we using ILWIS. Then we create polygon maps and convert to raster map.

Interviewer: What are a polygon map and a raster map?

Naveen: Polygon map is line map, like India river maps that we see. Raster maps are color or pixel maps. In atlas, for geographical map, it is overlay of polygon map on raster map.

(In the meanwhile, the interviewer has pulled up the ILWIS quick guide on his laptop; being a Photoshop expert, he understands a lot of stuff mentioned there.)

Interviewer: How do you rasterize the polygon map?

Naveen: ILWIS gives one option for that.

Interviewer: OK, what are the inputs needed for this option?

Naveen: Inputs? Polygon map is needed.

Interviewer: That's all?

Naveen (*nodding*): Yes.

Interviewer: What next?

Naveen: Then we creating Drastic model.

Interviewer: Hmm …

Naveen: We need rate of past 10 years for that.

(The interviewer quickly searches for drastic model and learns that it is "DRASTIC model" and is used for evaluating groundwater pollution potential. Now he is genuinely intrigued.)

Interviewer: Hmm …

Naveen: Soil use pattern for 10 years is needed also.

Interviewer: Wait Naveen, why are you "creating" DRASTIC model?

Naveen: For land use.

Interviewer: See, I am completely confused now. First you mention that you are studying your institute campus but don't mention the type of study. Then you talk about tourism and increase your study scope to the entire city. Now you talk about soil use and DRASTIC model. How are all these things related?

Naveen (*blank expression*)

Interviewer: And what services are you using to obtain the GPS location coordinate values?

Naveen: …

Interviewer: I will assume all that you have mentioned till now is somehow related. In that case, please tell me how are you collecting the 10-year data for soil use pattern?

Naveen: ...

Interviewer: What should I infer from that silence?

Naveen: We use ArcGIS also.

Interviewer: So?

Naveen: ArcGIS is also another software.

Interviewer: OK ...

Naveen: That's it about project.

Interviewer: OK then, Naveen. That's it from me also.

SCENE 3

The interviewer wastes no time in rejecting Naveen with the following comments:

Subject Knowledge – Poor

Project Description – Very Poor

Communication – Poor

Attitude – Bad

SCENE 4

The interviewer is not able to shake Naveen off his mind and is trying to find consolation in the fact that he has learnt two software names and three terms. He is trying to find out the reasons for him talking the way he did. At last he gets a conclusive impression:

"He would have definitely done some homework on the question regarding his comfort level with IT field and some intelligent person must have given him the idea of justifying his compatibility citing the experience using GIS software products. And he would have assumed that I would know nothing from that field. It was a fact till he mentioned names and I ran a quick search on them.

He has either done nothing for his project or his project is on some other topic and technology; he was trying to pass off a cocktail of small simple concepts and poor grammar as a real project. Come on, we are at least that much intelligent to see through so much of incoherence and catch the fakes.

God knows his competence at C; I was so pissed off that I did not care to check his C skills. How could I trust him on that anyways?

❋ ❋ ❋

20

Chemical's Harjeet Converses with Big Money exec

SCENE 1

Harjeet had brushed up his knowledge on the current economic topics and that provided him an edge over aggressive speakers in the group discussion. Now after clearing the GD round, he is confused about the questions that the BM execs might ask; they are a finance domain company with a strong in-house IT department. At the moment, the probability of questions from chemical, computer science, and economics domains looks equal to him. This confusion had also forced him study like crazy during the last one week. As he is called, he wishes that he is asked fewer questions on economics.

SCENE 2

Interviewer: Come in please, Harjeet! How are you?

Harjeet: I am fine, Sir, thank you.

Interviewer: You can take a seat!

Harjeet: Thank you, Sir.

Interviewer: Your resume says you are good at programming. Have you ever written a program to generate a sine wave output?

Harjeet (*bemused*): Sine … wave output?

Interviewer: Yes.

Harjeet: No, I have not done that. I have solved other pattern-making problems that are given in exercises.

Interviewer (*amused*): It's good for me that you haven't done it before! Can you do it now?

Harjeet: But Sir, that will take a lot of calculations and adjustments to get the wave shape. It cannot be done on paper; I need to run the program to see that.

Interviewer: Why?

Harjeet: The wave is symmetrical across the axis, and distance between the two 'X' points needs to be calculated because if the cursor goes to the next line once, it cannot be brought back to the previous line. Both the X points need to be displayed at the same time.

Diagram 1

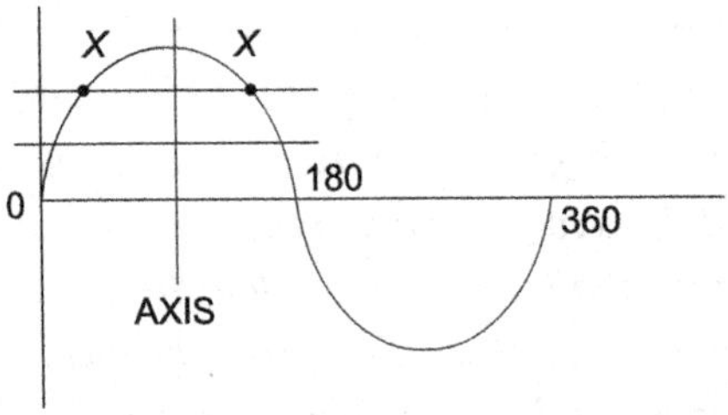

Interviewer: What if I turn the paper around like this?

Diagram 2

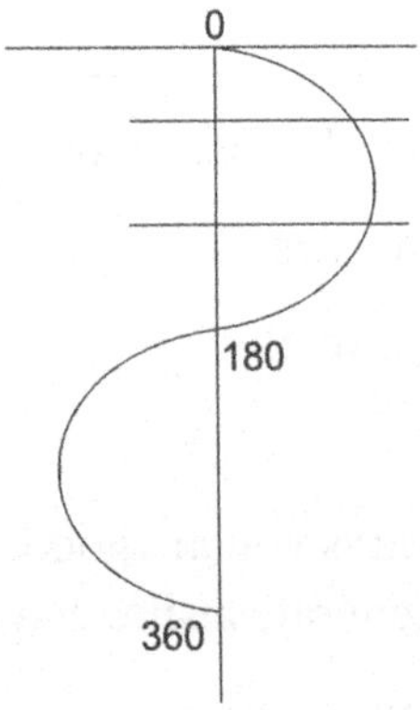

Harjeet: Yeah, now I can do it.

Interviewer: Can you briefly explain the approach you are going to follow?

Harjeet: Hmm...yeah, there should be two sections to the program. One section will generate the wave shape from 0 to 180 degrees. The output would look like

Diagram 3

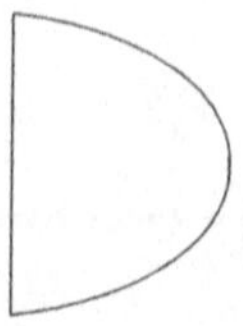

The second section has to generate the wave from 180 to 360 degrees.

Diagram 4

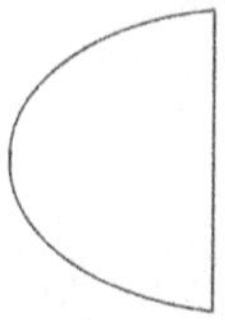

In fact, a third section is also required to work in conjunction with the first section to shift the entire wave to the right hand side to an extent that it aligns properly with the 180 to 360 degrees section.

Interviewer: How about the frequency and amplitude control?

Harjeet: I had not thought of that. Please give me sometime to work it out.

(Harjeet spends around 5 minutes thinking and scribbling logic and rejecting and modifying parts of it. Then he takes a few minutes to write the end-to-end program.)

```
/*****************************************************/

#include <iostream.h>

#include <math.h>

void main()
```

```
{
    double val, j, k, amp, step;
    cout <<"Enter step size in multiples of 10 for frequency \n";
    cin >> step;
    cout << "Enter amplitude in multiples of 0.05 \n";
    cin >> amp;
/*******************************************************/
    for (k=0; k<185;k+=step)
    {
/*******************************************************/
        for (j=0;j<=1;j+=amp)
            cout << " ";
/*******************************************************/
        val=sin(((k*(22/7))/180));

        for (j=0;j<=val;j+=amp)
        {
            cout << " ";
        }
        cout << "***\n";
    }
/*******************************************************/
    for (k=185; k>=0;k-=step)
      {
        val=sin(((k*(22/7))/180));

        for (j=0;j<=(1-val);j+=amp)
        {
            cout << " ";
        }
        cout << "***\n";
    }
```

```
}
/****************************************************/
```

Interviewer: Which lines correspond to which sections of the logic you had mentioned?

Harjeet: The for loop

```
for (j=0;j<=1;j+=amp)
```

shifts the upper part of the wave to the right side to align with the lower part. That's why it is a constant loop with a maximum value of 1, the highest value for sign function. That is also the maximum right to which the lower part of the wave can be displayed.

Then the for loop

```
for (j=0;j<=val;j+=amp)
```

forms the first section. It prints whitespaces depending on the wave amplitude at the moment and after this the character "***" is printed. As there is no new line between the earlier and this for loop, the wave starts forming from the offset generated by above.

The third for loop, for (j=0;j<=(1-val);j+=amp), generates the lower section of the wave. As it is inverted, I am using (1 - val) to get the inverted amplitude value.

Interviewer: How does the step size determine the frequency?

Harjeet: The step size determines the number of lines the wave is displayed over. So if we reduce the step size, more amplitude values will be calculated and take up more lines for display. That will reduce the frequency. But if the step size is bigger, that will mean fewer points will be displayed. As every point takes up one line, it will mean fewer lines or a narrower wave.

Interviewer: And how do you alter the amplitude?

Harjeet: By the same concept. The number of whitespaces is determined by the number of times the wave formation loop runs. If amplitude step size is smaller, that means more iteration, more whitespaces, and a bigger wave.

Interviewer: Very fine then. Tell me have you heard of Web 2.0?

Harjeet: It is the evolving and more interactive, rather than the plain informative, version of web. Blogs are an example where the users have a lot of interactive control.

Interviewer: What are friends?

Harjeet: Hmm … friends … friends are good people.

Interviewer (*laughing*): True, but have you heard of friends in programming?

Harjeet (*smiling*): Oh, so sorry, you mean friend functions and classes in C++?

Interviewer (*smiling*): Yup!

Harjeet: Suppose an object F is declared as a friend of another object B. In that case F will get access to the private and protected members of B. This is the friend concept. A function or a class can be declared as a friend by preceding its declaration by the keyword friend.

Interviewer: Can you write a quick program to explain this?

Harjeet: Yea, I can do that.

```
/*****************************************************/
#include <iostream.h>

class B {
    int var1;
    private:
        int var2;
        void priv()
        {cout << "\nValues are: " << var1 << " " << var2 << " " << var3;};
    public:
        int var3;
        void show()
        {cout << "\nValues are: " << var1 << " " << var2 << " " << var3;};
    friend void F(int, int);
};
```

```
/******************************************************/
void F(int a, int b)
{
        B BVal;
        BVal.var1 = a;
        BVal.var2 = b;
        BVal.var3 = 0;
        BVal.show();
        BVal.priv();
}
/******************************************************/
void test(int a, int b)
{
        B BVal1;
        //BVal1.var1 = a;
        //BVal1.var2 = b;
        BVal1.var3 = 5;
        BVal1.show();
        //BVal1.priv();
}
/******************************************************/
void main ()
{
        test(3,4);
        F(1,2);
}
/******************************************************/
```

Harjeet: The data members "var1" and "var2" and the method "priv()" are generally not accessible outside the base class B. But since method F has been declared as a friend, it can access these variables directly.

The method "test()" is not a friend; hence, it cannot access these variables. If it tries to access, it will give compilation error.

Interviewer: I think "test()" can access these members of A if you declare "test()" as a friend of F, isn't it?

Harjeet: No, Sir, it does not work like that. A would still not consider "test()" as a friend function.

Interviewer: My program has to accept a console input "Hello program, I am happy you read me." Can you help me on this?

Harjeet: Sure, Sir. As it is a space-separated string, the "cin" extraction operator ">>" won't work. Getline() function can be used for that.

```
/******************************************************/
#include <iostream.h>
#include <string.h>

void main ()
{
        string test;
        cout << "\nEnter a string\n";
        getline (cin, test);
        cout << "\n" << test << "\n";
}
/******************************************************/
```

Interviewer: All right Harjeet. Let me enter a string:

"That was the last question I had for you! Thank you very much for your time."

Harjeet (*smiling*): Thank you, Sir. Bye.

SCENE 3

Harjeet is pleasantly surprised at the low difficulty level of the questions asked and is almost thinking that there was no need to put in so much of efforts for the preparation. As per his expectations, the interviewer declares him as a Final Select.

Programming Skills – Very Good

IQ – High

Communication – Very Good

Attitude – Very Good

SCENE 4

On learning that Harjeet has been selected, colleagues ask the interviewer how he could make a favorable decision on someone so soon for a change this time.

The interviewer discloses that Harjeet had happened to be a part of the group discussion he had moderated. He had already got a good glimpse of his soft skills and general awareness by his GD performance and there was no need to test that again. So all he had to judge on now was his programming aptitude and IQ.

He further adds that the guy was really good and thorough at programming. He wrote really simple and straightforward code. He could write a perfect code for sine wave display, including waveform shape and amplitude and frequency change during the interview though it could be seen that he had not done it before. To explain the "friend member" concept, he wrote a few lines and included both scenarios, as to what would happen when a member was friend and when a member was not a friend. And he really liked that. So he opines that the credit for a quick closure should really go to Harjeet!

* * *

Author's Profile

Deepa Jain is a gold medalist in Electronics and Communication Engineering from NIT Bhopal. She has been working with IBM India in the Data Warehousing and Business Intelligence (DWBI) domain since 2005. She likes interviewing people and has been doing so for the last 5 years.

Made in the USA
Monee, IL
04 November 2026

67379308R00134